TOM BENNETT

THE RUNNING THE ROOM COMPANION

ISSUES IN CLASSROOM MANAGEMENT AND STRATEGIES TO DEAL WITH THEM

First Published 2021

by John Catt Educational Ltd,
15 Riduna Park, Station Road,
Melton, Woodbridge IP12 1QT

Tel: +44 (0) 1394 389850
Email: enquiries@johncatt.com
Website: www.johncatt.com

ISBN: 978 1 913622 40 4

Set and designed by John Catt Educational Limited

PRAISE FOR *RUNNING THE ROOM*

When Tom Bennett writes, common sense leaps off the page and slaps you in the face. You will find yourself engrossed, helplessly nodding in total agreement as he shares his years of research, experience and first-hand accounts from schools. It is hard to imagine anyone reading this book and not improving their thinking and day-to-day classroom practice.

Tom's tales will engage and amuse you, the practical advice will inspire you, but most importantly this book will change the way you think about school culture and its impact on pupil behaviour.

Damian McBeath,
Regional Director for Ark Schools, London and Portsmouth

In this masterful volume, Bennett outlines the highest-impact theories and strategies to be able to – as it says on the tin – run the room. Bad advice is everywhere when it comes to behaviour, and no other book explains easily actionable and effective techniques so clearly. This is the book I needed years ago; how much time have I wasted discovering for myself a fraction of the techniques and routines clearly outlined in this book? Readers are indeed lucky to have access to it as I have no doubt it will improve the practice of teachers with all levels of experience.

Adam Boxer, Chemistry teacher,
Editor of *The researchED Guide to Explicit and Direct Instruction*

Wise, clear, and eminently practical, this book will help teachers create a classroom atmosphere where students feel valued and ready to work.

Professor Daniel Willingham,
Professor of Psychology at the University of Virginia

Running the Room is a unique book. It's a rare combination of erudition and anecdote, gravity and wit, failures and triumphs, self-deprecation and swank, trials and tribulations and optimism. In a style that often made me think of Samuel Clemens (Mark Twain), Tom shows us how running the room is the teacher's ultimate act of love and dedication to education and their students.

Professor Paul Kirschner,
Emeritus Professor of Educational Psychology and Guest Professor,
Thomas More University of Applied Science

In some areas of education, there is lots of high-quality research evidence about the 'best bets' for improving one's practice. For these areas, my advice is simple: read the research and figure out what this might mean for your own practice. In other areas, like behaviour management, where the research evidence is thin, weak, or contradictory, my advice is different, but equally simple. Find people who know what they are talking about, and listen to what they have to say. Like Tom Bennett.

In *Running the Room*, Tom condenses all he has learned about managing student behaviour – from his experiences as an inner-city school teacher, by observing hundreds (thousands?) of classrooms, and by carefully researching what good research there is – into a wonderfully accessible, practical – and, yes, funny – guide to classroom management. This book is the best guide I have ever read on getting good behaviour in classrooms. It should be required reading for those training to teach, but experienced teachers will also find a lot here to reflect on, and to use. Highly recommended.

Dylan Wiliam,
Emeritus Professor, University College London

'Practical' is the standard praise for a book on behaviour, but Bennett's book is something different: a thing of beauty. And not just because of his humility, humor and occasionally elegiac prose. Because the truth is beautiful. To love children is to ensure that our classrooms protect them and honor their chance at learning – bring out the best in each of them and teach them to be giving and positive members of the society we share. Sadly the first response when adults find themselves unable to ensure such an outcome is often to argue that it is unnecessary. Rarely has anyone explained so clearly an alternative and provided as practical (and beautiful) a guide to accomplishing it.

Doug Lemov,
Author of *Teach Like a Champion*

I cannot stop quoting Tom Bennett's *Running the Room*. I bought this because everyone said it was incredible, and everyone was absolutely correct. I'm not sure how he manages it, but Bennett makes this a relevant read for both practitioners at the very start of their careers and those leading the behaviour and culture of schools.

Jo Facer,
Headteacher

To Anna, Gabriella and Ben, my true loves
To Anthony, the World's Finest brother and best friend
And to my parents, Tom and Elizabeth, always

CONTENTS

THE PRINCIPLES OF THE CLASSROOM

These principles underpin everything I have learned about excellent classroom management. Some of them may seem obvious, some of them may seem ambiguous. Throughout this book I will refer or allude to these principles, and my hope is that by the end, they will make sense, seem sensible, and make a difference in your own understanding. Which, with luck, will direct your behaviour, and that of your students.

1. **Behaviour is a curriculum**
2. **Children must be taught how to behave**
3. **Teach, don't tell, behaviour**
4. **Make it easy to behave and hard not to**
5. **No one behaviour strategy will work with all students**
6. **Relationships are built on trust, which is built on structure**
7. **Students are social beings**
8. **Consistency is the foundation of all good habits**
9. **Everyone wants to matter**
10. **My room, my rules**

Tom Bennett

Si vis pacem, para bellum.

If you want peace, prepare for war.

BEHAVIOUR IS A CURRICULUM

Being well-behaved is a combination of skills, aptitudes, habits, inclinations, values, and knowledge. These can be taught.

INTRODUCTION

If I have seen further, it is by standing on the shoulders of Giants.
Isaac Newton, 1675

Standing on the shoulders of giants

This book originally began life as an annexe of its predecessor, *Running the Room: The Teacher's Guide to Behaviour*. But that book grew like Jack's beanstalk underneath my fingertips, smashing through the ceiling of a healthy or bearable word count. 'In writing,' William Faulkner allegedly said, 'you must kill all your darlings.'[1] That's a fine principle, in principle. Years of writing copy for newspapers and magazines to deadline, to length, taught me a lot about the merciless execution of redundant prose. There is a time for ornamentation, and a time for economy. Orwell's six rules of good writing stress 'if it is possible to cut a word out, always cut it out'.[2]

And this is irrefutably true. But I am also reminded of the aphorism that advises us to 'say things as simply as possible – but no simpler'.[3] As the book grew and grew, I realised I had more to say than I thought. As I examined every topic, they needed room to breathe and grow and lay down roots. I pruned and pollarded, but there came a point when I no longer wanted to; when what was gained by economy and brevity seemed to detract from both the skeleton and the skin of the book's intent.

---

1   By now, of course, whenever we hear a famous aphorism, we should expect it to be falsely attributed. In fact, this was said by the writer Sir Arthur Quiller-Couch: 'Whenever you feel an impulse to perpetrate a piece of exceptionally fine writing, obey it – wholeheartedly – and delete it before sending your manuscript to press. Murder your darlings.'

2   Can you imagine how much better this paragraph would be if I had listened to this advice?

3   'Everything should be made as simple as possible, but no simpler,' is a quote semi-attributed to Einstein by Roger Sessions in the New York Times in 1950. What he actually said was less poetic and compact, and Sessions probably paraphrased for a more elegant effect. www.bit.ly/3qaynFL

No doubt I got it wrong, as authors have done since cuneiform. We all believe nothing can be cut. But the film on the floor made a movie of its own. And that is what, more or less, you hold in your hand. The director's off-cuts.

In my previous book, *Running the Room: the Teacher's Guide to Behaviour,* I discussed the principles, philosophies and theory underpinning behaviour in classrooms. I also dug deeply into the systems and habits that *teachers* need to develop in order for *children* to develop the habits that help them to succeed in school and beyond.

Throughout that book, I tried to be as practical as possible. Teachers do not need yet more gaseous, ineffective theory that leads them into contemplation and no more. Fine ideas alone won't settle a year 9 class when a bee buzzes in through the window. Teachers need suggestions about what to do and what to say in the face of the most common challenges students offer.

In this companion guide, I summarise some of the most effective strategies and responses to these challenges by drawing on successful practice I've seen. In the past decade, I must have been to around 300–400 schools, specifically to look at their behaviour systems. I have observed hundreds of classrooms, and magpied the best of what I saw without mercy, paying particular attention to when strategies surprised me, or ran contrary to my expectations. Our biases are to some extent baked in, but the least we can do is reflect more generously on what doesn't fit with our beliefs. I have asked teachers and students what they think works best, and why, and triangulated that with what I have observed. These are the giants upon whose shoulders I have stood.

None of these strategies are incontrovertible, or irrefutable; all of them are practical templates for what you might do in your own classroom. Treat them like chords; learn them and play jazz; jam with them or make jam. It's entirely up to you. Running a room is like making a crowd laugh. There are few absolute rules, but lots of best bets about what people will find funny. And there are lots of things that will depend on the audience.

You may have strategies of your own to add to these. Good. Every teacher has the right to add to the sum total of professional experience that makes up the body of professional knowledge towards which we aspire. But it is absurd for us to expect teachers to reinvent these skills every generation. It is essential that we share these strategies, not as 'best practice' or anything so utopian. But by looking over the shoulders of those who have gone before us, we can copy each other's essays, correct their mistakes, and hand in homework that our successors can marvel at as it hangs upon the wonderwalls of our intergenerational story. We stand on one another's shoulders.

The parable of the gardens

Two brothers each inherited a garden. One brother's garden was a jungle, dark and overgrown with weeds and grasses and bushes and thick sprouting plants. A few old trees grew here and there, with heavy trunks burying roots deep in the soil. Parts of it were wet and marshy where your feet sank down to the knee. Other parts were sandy and dry. The ground rose up into small hillocks and sank down unevenly in waves and ridges. Worse, it stood all alone, miles from anywhere. All it had was a fence around it to say that it belonged to anyone at all.

The second brother's garden could not have been more different. It was flat and even; all the weeds had long since been eliminated. The soil was turned thoroughly. It was not too sandy, not too damp. It had been tilled and ploughed. It got lots of light, and the fence around it kept it safe from the strongest winds. It stood at the end of a neat house, and the house stood next door to a garden centre, which stood next to a vegetable shop.

Both brothers loved to garden, and both had the same simple ambition: they wanted to grow things – beautiful flowers, ripe vegetables and fruit.

The first brother barely knew where to start. He tried to weed the garden, but there were so many of them, it felt like he would never end. He looked at the tree trunks and wondered how he would even cut them down, let alone dig out those enormous roots. The marshes needed draining, and that was going to take weeks. The ground would need to be turned and tilled and dug by an army; it would need fertiliser, and more tilling, and finally flattening with a roller.

Even getting tools to the garden was difficult because it was so remote. There was barely a road within miles, so everything had to be carried to the gate. Where he lived, tools were expensive, and poor quality. He had to search far and wide to find the seeds he needed, and every time he wanted to visit the garden, it took him a day of travelling there and back. Meanwhile, he had other things to do: a job, a family, responsibilities. Some days he woke up and thought, 'I can't be bothered with this today,' and went back to bed.

The second brother simply popped next door to the garden centre and planted the seeds he needed in a day. He lived close, so it was easy to drop in to water the ground, dig out any weeds. The soil was so good, things were growing in no time.

So which gardener would be more successful? Which garden?

If we follow the conventions of this parable, it's an easy answer: the second brother and garden. Everything is geared up for their mutual success. The conditions are just right for things to grow. A lot of the work appears to have been done already by some kind predecessor. Planting and looking after the seeds is as easy as possible. Crucially, there are as few impediments to success as the universe can manage.

Is it *impossible* for the first brother to succeed? Of course not. I know gardeners who would thrill to the challenge of this. I know people who would camp out in the garden and spend their whole waking life attacking it, breaking its back, dragging it into shape day by day. It is entirely *possible* for the first brother to succeed.

But is it more *likely*? Of course not. Were you to take a thousand people and give them the first garden, and another thousand and give them the second garden, which group would on average see more success? Of course, the second. Some in the first group would succeed, but it is very likely that, on average, people in the first scenario would do fractionally as well as the second group, for lots of good reasons.

I use this parable to teach the difference in challenge that teachers face. If you are fortunate to teach fortunate children in fortunate circumstances, then you may find behaviour a marginal problem. You may even be unable to understand why some people make such a fuss about it. You may even start to believe that you have some magical gift for managing behaviour that others do not possess. You may even start to make unrealistic but superficially convincing arguments about what teachers in less fortunate circumstances need to do in order to achieve the same quality of behaviour you enjoy. Imagine a school advisor, fresh from ten years behind a desk, subsequent to a decade in a top private school, coming into your lesson and telling you, 'You just need to inspire them a bit more.'

Teachers in less fortunate circumstances dealing with high levels of challenge may suffer different issues. They may think themselves inadequate. They may leave the profession, exhausted. They may learn to accept poor behaviour and poor learning as inevitable.

You never achieve perfect behaviour. It is a Sisyphean battle to constantly improve the behaviour you have, to prevent its decay, to continually build. It is a garden. It requires constant maintenance. You will fight many battles over and over. You will lose some of them. But persistence and structure will defeat all but the most intractable of circumstances. It is one of the most important aspects of the job, and that job is one of the most important in the world. It is a struggle that is very worth having, because the fruits of it are so extraordinary.

Good luck
Tom

Summary of *Running the Room*

For a full exploration of the basics of classroom management, see *Running the Room*, to which this is a companion text.[4] To offer some brief context, here is a summary of the story so far...

- Children are largely the products of their circumstances. They do not invent themselves, and their character, habits, knowledge, inclinations and behaviour are very strongly influenced by their environments. Children who are polite, patient, and hardworking have often absorbed these patterns of behaviour from their parents, their previous educational settings, their families, their peers, their immediate cultures. Children who are impatient, demanding, argumentative and prone to loafing have probably had these traits cultivated by the same factors.

- This means that children who arrive in your classroom didn't spring into existence as they enter; they are the sum of their pasts. Some of them are inclined to behave in ways we might say are useful to be a good student, and some of them do so in a way that is positively toxic to that aim. But we call the former a good student, and congratulate them, and the latter a bad one, and reprimand them. And perhaps we still should.

---

4   And by 'see' I of course mean 'purchase ten copies'.

- But unless we accept that the behaviour they need to flourish as students can be learned, and therefore taught, we treat them as if they know how to behave the way we want but choose not to. And sometimes that is true. But often we ask them to behave in ways that we would find hard ourselves were we not used to doing it.

- Behaviour must be taught. Teachers and the school must teach them behaviour they don't have in order to help them to flourish as students and human beings. So, behaviour is like a curriculum. And like any curriculum, there are good and bad ways to teach it. What we mustn't do is simply tell them to 'behave' and then praise or punish them according to their output. First, we patiently teach the behaviour, like any practical skill or academic syllabus. We check for common misconceptions. We ask them to demonstrate the learning. We reteach what has not been learned. We revise. And so on.

- Teachers must be conscious architects of the classroom culture – the beliefs and values that underpin the group. And understanding groups is very important to the teacher, because students, like all humans, are social animals: we react to other people's behaviour all the time; we look for their cues in order to know how to act; we need to feel we belong to groups. Status matters. Esteem matters. We need to feel valued, and valuable, and meaningful.

- That quest for meaning leads some students to misbehave, because they see what is normal and feel drawn to it in order to be accepted by the group. If lateness is normal, many students will try not to be conspicuously early so as to stand out and risk social exclusion. So social norms can reinforce misbehaviour, but they can also reinforce good behaviour if the teacher takes a firm control of what is normal for the classroom. They need to constantly promote and communicate normative messages and, crucially, challenge students who transgress these norms.

- These norms are also communicated through the efficient use of systematically taught routines, i.e. sequences of learned behaviour, such as entry routines, activity transition routines and so on. Norms and routines are the building blocks of this proactive phase of behaviour management. It should be the priority of every teacher to focus on this phase, rather than simply relying constantly on reactions and consequences to behaviour, good or otherwise. That said, consequences still matter. The reactive phase of behaviour management is crucial too, because it reinforces the norms established in the proactive phase. Without them, the proactive phase will only affect some students, sometimes. But the knowledge that actions have consequences, good or bad, for the student will help to maintain the norms the teacher has patiently created and communicated.

- Finally, a word on the teacher-pupil relationship. Every teacher must confront the responsibility of their position. It is an adult role; it is a mentor role; it is a teacher's role. We do not enter into a relationship of equals with the children. They do not need another tall friend. They need an adult who will assume responsibility for their safety, their dignity and their flourishing. We do not ask permission to run the room; we run the room because we must. Because the alternative is that the room runs us; because when we defer the responsibility to do so, the children run the room instead. And it is a brave and optimistic person who would claim that children would make a better, fairer fist of it than a trained adult. It's your room, and these are your rules, directed to the benefit of all.

In the rest of this book we will explore in more detail some of the more common situations a teacher will face in his or her career. For a job with so much diversity, there is a great deal of similarity between the challenges teachers face, across the ages and stages. That might be something to do with the fact that we are all human beings, and deep down, perhaps we are not so different after all.[5]

---

5   Powers, Douglas

CHILDREN MUST BE TAUGHT HOW TO BEHAVE

Being well behaved is not an accident of birth. Students do not create themselves. We are all the products of our circumstances. Students who behave well have been taught these things already. If they have not, the teacher must try to do so.

CHAPTER 1
'MAKE ME': SUGGESTION, PERSUASION, AND COMPULSION

How do we change behaviour? It's at the centre of everything we try to do in the classroom: to make students choose to perform one action (e.g. complete a maths worksheet) rather than another (e.g. draw erupting cartoon phalluses on the desk in correction fluid).

The COVID-19 crisis of 2020 offers us an interesting case study. Across the world, governments of every stripe were faced with a colossal challenge: in the face of a global pandemic, how do you move entire nations to change their behaviour in order to minimise further catastrophe? I'll focus on the UK, although similar stories unfolded elsewhere.

Initially, before each country was hit with the first big wave of the virus, there was a very low level of concern from many people and their governments. Why *should* we change our behaviour? There didn't seem to be much point. We'd seen other viruses before – SARS, swine flu, bird flu etc. – and in those examples, the behavioural change of the average person was probably quite limited in countries like the UK, because their chances of being affected directly were very low.

Another issue is that for many people, the kind of behaviour we were being asked to change seemed so trivial. Take hand washing, or respiratory hygiene. One of the reasons that we've made so many advances in health in the last few centuries has been simple mechanical behavioural habits like hand washing after visiting the toilet, routine washing on a daily basis, cleaning schedules at home and in commercial premises, sanitation, plumbing, building design, and so on.

In fact, it can get to the point that, for the average person, we forget why we do such things, and start to see them as cosmetic and social functions: we don't want to smell and so on. Of course, there are always those for whom such things are more than niceties: the chronically ill, those with suppressed immunities, health care professionals, sanitation workers etc., those for whom there was a clear and present danger that only high levels of hygiene could combat.

But everyone else? Viruses are a good example of a risk that is poorly grasped because they are invisible to us and their effects can seem so remote. Infection and incubation can take a while to lead to symptoms, if they do at all. We all know how differently people adhere to cleanliness routines. A trip on any Tube, bus or rush hour train can confirm the breadth and complexity of how closely each person understands intimate hygiene. Levels also vary between groups: men and women, for example, have well-documented differences in adherence to social demands about cleanliness,[6] which is probably explained by different social attitudes towards hygiene by gender.

And then something happens to change the status quo; in this case, a global pandemic of a virus with no vaccine, with high transmissibility and a significant fatality rate, steeped in unknowns. The advice for societies at large was eventually very similar to previous outbreaks: social isolation to prevent cross-contamination; renewed and substantially improved personal hygiene, particularly hands; suppressing large groups; preventing all but essential travel; and so on. And at its height, lockdowns and the almost complete cessation of everyday life.

So, we suddenly had a global experiment in *what* motivates people, *who* is motivated, and *when*. Governments all over the world scrambled to change behaviour profoundly, at a scale rarely seen outside of wartime, in some of the most deeply ingrained areas of our behaviour, habits, cultures and identities. And not just for short periods of time or small targeted groups, but for almost everyone, almost everywhere, for a sustained period of time.

Governments everywhere were telling their citizens to change their customs and habits enormously, suddenly, through press, TV, daily briefings, posters and adverts. It was a mass-marketing campaign with a multibillion-dollar budget.

So, what happened? Well, to a large extent, the results weren't that surprising.

- Some people didn't need to change their behaviour because they were already doing the right thing, e.g. ICU nurses. If anything, they doubled down, led by professional domain expertise, existing habits and institutional edict.

---

6   Jackson, C. and Newall, M. (2018) Hygiene and Cleanliness in the U.S., Ipsos. www.bit.ly/2UUESOu

- Some people took heed immediately and made the fastest behavioural changes. These would typically be people inspired by altruism, concern for others, concern for their own health, people who already believed hygiene was important, the fearful or paranoid, or those who were the most compliant and conformist to social norms.

- The next group changed their behaviour somewhat but did so reluctantly. For some, they believed the threat was more remote. Others had the sense that the virus wouldn't affect them personally, only others. For some, the understanding that it predominantly affected other age groups meant that their initial motivation was low. For others yet, it was the sense that this was just another flu epidemic, and how bad was the flu really? For some it was mistrust of the authorities. For others it was laziness. For some it was being too busy to focus, or too concerned with other areas of their lives. For some, it was fatalism or weltschmerz. And so on.

- The last group were the hardliners. These were the people who wouldn't change their behaviours despite any number of health campaigns, press briefings, public information campaigns, requests, nudges or persuasion. They either didn't believe there was a threat, believed the threat didn't touch them, or were incapable or unwilling to amend their habits for the benefit of others. Some believed internet hoaxes that spun lies about the origin or nature of the pandemic. Some were too motivated by opportunity to do so; some followed demagogues, politicians and fanatical leaders who soothed their fears with comforting lies. These people couldn't be persuaded by argument, reason, asking; they only responded to legal or economic threats: penalties, fines, incarceration or some other practical consequences. And some defied even these systematic warnings.

The point is that whenever behavioural change is required in any group, expect the following:

- Some people will happily embrace the change, and simply need to be asked or instructed to do so.

- Some people need to have the change explained to them, and perhaps some assistance with making the changes, but will do so readily once these criteria are met.

- Some people need the reasons explained over and over, will wait to see if other people are doing it, and will revert easily back to old habits unless constant reminders are given.

- Some people will change with great reluctance, and need to know that short-term positive or negative consequences will result from participating or not with their social norms.

- Some people will only respond in the face of certain sanction.

- Some people will still not respond to the stimulus, even in the face of that sanction, even when the case is made repeatedly and assistance is offered to do so.

This is another way of saying that people are people, and not everyone is the same. People often respond differently to the exact same stimulus. Obvious, perhaps, but a truism whose simplicity is often overlooked in programmes of behavioural change. You can't simply present stimulus X to group Y and expect uniform response Z. If you give a menu to 20 diners, don't expect them all to order the Caesar salad.

Imagine the list above mapped onto the classroom:

- Some students will do what you want before you've finished asking. They already know the kind of behaviour you want, they can do it, and they're happy to do it.

- Some students already have a good idea about what they should be doing, and just need a minor nudge to remind them, or to activate the behaviours. Or they know but find it a little tricky and need you to teach them a little how to do it.

- Some children will be prepared to try to do what you want, but you may need to explain what that means in great detail or support them to do so in many ways.

- Some children will really struggle to do what you want even if you explain it well and they are capable of doing so and will need some form of constant behaviour feedback or consequential system to motivate them even more explicitly.

- Some children will refuse to do what you want no matter what the consequence or quality of instruction, or their ability to do it.

The summary of this is that people choose to behave for lots of different reasons, and in order to motivate them to behave in a certain way, it is necessary to consider a magazine of approaches or a repertoire of strategies to do so, rather than expect one simple approach to work equally on all students.

Three ways teachers change behaviour

In *Running the Room*, we discussed why some people feel uncomfortable 'telling' someone what to do. 'Making' others behave the way we want presents us with some perfectly reasonable questions. What right do we have to do so? What limits our rights to make others behave how we wish? What does the relationship between those issuing instructions and those expected to comply look like? And what dangers and opportunities does all this present?

I strongly advocate this principle: *my room, my rules*. The teacher needs to be the adult authority of the room and do so without hesitation or uncertainty. They need to embrace this aspect of their role, or they will undermine themselves constantly with indecisiveness. Teachers must reserve the right to be in charge and demonstrate this constantly by their actions and words. The justification for this comes not from power or ideology, but from necessity. If the teacher is not in charge, the children are.

In my experience, a great deal of criticism aimed at this approach comes from a squeamishness about telling others what to do. If any teacher feels this way, I applaud them. No one should enjoy telling others what to do. Although we might find giving instructions becomes easier with repetition, we should resist the temptation that command should be pleasant or fun. Such an expectation can lead us into the pursuit of power for its own sake, which is a corruption of its intrinsic aim. Those following this path will abuse their power for their own ends or the continuity of their position, and by doing so relinquish the right to lead.

But reluctance to assume the necessary role of authority is often born of a misunderstanding about how we lead and how we direct the behaviour of others. We do not simply *compel* students to behave as we wish. Or rather, that is only a small part of what we do. In reality, there are at least three increasing levels of insistence.

The three levels of insistence

Think of how you 'make' other people behave in your everyday life.

Example:

I get up in the morning, or rather, my children get me up.[7] I ask them if they would enjoy playing quietly by themselves for a while until Daddy's eyelids unglue. They assure me that they would not prefer this. I suggest to them that if they go to the bathroom first, I'll get up and make them some Daddy toast (which is just toast and jam but is apparently attractive because it's what I have and therefore is a symbol of maturity and independence). Off they trot. We watch some *Scooby-Doo* together and then I ask them to go upstairs. Then I ask again, and then a few times more. Then the TV goes off and I mention that they're going to be late and have to stand at the back of the line in school when they get in. The eldest does not want this to happen and dashes upstairs to get dressed. Her little brother trots after her, happily.

Once upstairs, there is a familiar routine of teeth, faces and hands, hair, dressing and so on. My daughter falls into this easily enough but needs reminders to keep going and not be distracted by the great 21st-century rabbit novel she's writing. My son needs more than a nudge, and I usually have to pick him up and start dressing him whether he likes it or not. Eventually he says he can dress himself like a big boy and spurns further assistance.

After about a hundred years of this, they're ready to roll. We walk smartly out together, and without being asked, they take my hands, and we walk, happy as clams, to school. They might spot a crop of conkers, and before I can stop them, they're scooping the treasure into their pockets until I intervene and suggest a limit to their acquisition. At the school gates they wait until I say my farewell mantra ('Have fun, work hard, learn lots, be kind') and then they dash off, keen to see their friends.

After that, I have ten minutes before I need to get back home and start work, so I turn into the local coffee shop and grab a flat white. I ask the barista for one and she hands it to me without dispute.[8]

---

7   At the time of writing I have two practically perfect children aged 4 and 7, which is to say I haven't needed an alarm clock for seven years.

8   There are worse ways to start the day.

24

Now consider the ways in which I 'directed' other people's behaviour in that short example. After a moment's thought, it becomes obvious that I barely 'made' my children behave the way I wanted, in the sense that I magically compelled them to do so. Mostly I asked them to do as I asked, or I nagged them to do it, and they realised I wouldn't stop until they did. Some things they wanted to do, and some took a little effort. Only very rarely did I force them to do it, e.g. by scooping up my little boy and dressing him.

We often hear this aphorism: *You can't control anyone other than yourself.* It's true. The only mind you control is your own.[9] What we really do is behave in ways that we hope will cause others to behave in the way we want. Anyone tempted to behave like Max von Sydow's priest in *The Exorcist*, bellowing 'The power of Christ compels you!', should be ready for disappointment. We do not have this ability.[10] We are not Professor X. The students are not Manchurian candidates.

It's much more accurate to say that we provide incentives for people to behave in ways we want, and then they react according to the dictates of their character and circumstances. 'Making' someone behave is rarely a violent or coercive act in everyday human interactions. It usually involves getting someone to behave the way you want because they decide it to be the best action in the circumstances. They may not even be aware any kind of compulsion has occurred.

Here are three big levels of pressure by which we affect the behaviour of others: *suggestion, persuasion*, and *compulsion*.

1. SUGGESTION – ASK THEM TO BEHAVE THE WAY YOU WANT.

'An idea put forward for consideration' which is then adopted by the students. One of the best ways to direct another's behaviour is simply to point out to them what behaviour you would like and see how they respond. If they comply, it is because they were already happy to do so, knew how to do it, and simply needed a prompt to begin. For example, in the classroom you put your fingers on your lips and some children respond by becoming quiet. They already know what it means. They want to start the lesson. They're keen to hear what you have to say.

---

9   If that. The question of free will is a rabbit hole too deep for us to dive into here. But my favourite niche in the debate is broadly the position offered by David Hume. He suggested that in order for us to meaningfully say we acted freely it might in fact be *necessary for all of our actions to have prior causes*, on the grounds that an uncaused action is not free, but chaotic.

10   And if you do, your lessons must be interesting.

Suggestion is the lightest-touch way to change someone's behaviour, because it requires you, the actor, to make the least effort in order to change their, the agent's, behaviour. It can seem easy because they already think what you have suggested is a good idea: it already chimes with their values and ambitions, and they can see the benefit of falling into line. It may be that they enjoy behaving in the way you indicate they should, or they may simply enjoy the outcomes of the behaviour. Or they are used to doing it. Telling a student who really likes history and really likes hearing you talk about it that they need to get started on some history is pushing an open door. Asking the barista to sell you a coffee is not the hardest task in the world.

Example:

In restaurants, I worked on commission; you sold more, you earned more. This incentivised staff to be pushy, recommending things people didn't want or need in order to accrue some meagre salary increase. For someone like me who hated hard selling, this presented a moral dilemma. How to be a good salesperson and also be someone who could look at themselves in the mirror at the end of the day? My answer was to learn the menu backwards, and then to help guide customers to choices that they didn't know they wanted but needed help to discover. People scan large menus quickly, stick to what they always have, and play safe under pressure. If you can find out what kind of things they like and then locate something they never knew they would like, you've done them a service. Sometimes that meant a lower-cost product, sometimes a higher one. But it usually meant a happier customer, which was good for the restaurant and good for the tip tray, which was where the real money was to be made, not the scraps gnawed from the dry bones of commission, where the house always won.

Influencing by suggestion requires that the recipients are already prepared to behave in the ways you want. You just have to wave the idea under their noses. Often we see children who are 'school ready': they are already patient, kind, hard-working and so on. These children are frequently biddable and compliant to sensible instructions. But the qualities that made them like this have already been baked in by their prior life experiences, home culture, previous school phase, etc. They come to school preprogrammed to do well.

This is why some people think that behaviour management is easy, or they 'can't see what the fuss is all about'. They are usually the fortunate beneficiaries of a classroom where most of the children have been highly prepared to operate successfully in a classroom environment. This might be down to socioeconomic factors, good fortune, low rates of special needs, or even that the school may be very good at creating a whole-school culture of good behaviour. Some fortunate teachers think behaviour management is easy because the conditions in which they work are less onerous than others. A skier going downhill will find it easier than one skiing uphill, but only a fool would congratulate the former for travelling further and faster than the latter in the same time.

The takeaway for the teacher is that one of the first things teachers must do is explicitly and clearly communicate what behaviour is expected of students in the classroom. With some students, this is all it will take to get them to behave the way you want. The big mistake many teachers make is to assume that children know the behaviour you want, or don't need it to be spelled out because it is obvious. Obvious to you, perhaps, but in *Running the Room* we discussed at length the problem of the curse of expertise. Never assume a student knows how to behave until you have evidence that they can. Until then, tell them and, better still, teach them.

Teaching students how to behave is one of the easiest ways of introducing desirable behaviour to students, because they understand what you mean, and how to do what you expect.

2. PERSUASION – SELL THE INTRINSIC BENEFITS OF BEHAVING WELL.
Introducing behaviour direction isn't enough for some. They need to be persuaded. They want to see what is in it for them. Many people struggle to focus effort on a task for long periods. That's perfectly understandable – hard work is hard. It can feel unpleasant, and it's natural to avoid unpleasant feelings where we can. But much of what we want students to do in school is not immediately pleasant. Studying, thinking hard, focusing and persisting with difficult tasks are not obviously fun activities. So we need to try to make students see either why the activity might eventually be enjoyable if they persist, or that their persistence will help them to obtain some future gain that will be enjoyable or important. In other words, you need to help students see the intrinsic *and* the extrinsic value of the activity.

Note that I say 'enjoyable or important'. Not everything we value is *pleasant*. Not everyone finds going to the gym enjoyable but we might appreciate the value of doing it during or after the activity. It may not be pleasant, but it is valuable. Of course there *are* many people who *do* enjoy the gym, which makes it a lot easier for them to stay fit. Telling a hungry diner to have the salad instead of the steak isn't always going to work if what they really, really want is the filet drowned in a peppercorn sauce with a side of triple-fried chips. But telling them that they're doing great on their diet, they're looking good, and they'll feel much better afterwards because they won't feel bloated or whatever is a much better way to convince someone to want a different outcome to the one they originally wanted.

Persuasion can be done in many ways. You can:

- **Focus on effective pedagogy.** When students understand and can complete their work, they are far more likely to try it. When they start to make connections between topics, ideas and skills, they start to feel competent. The sensation of being 'good at something' is very addictive. Feeling like you can do something is much more enticing than feeling unable to do it. I remember at school, I used to love learning, because I thought learning was possible, and it was just a matter of thinking hard and trying. I see now how valuable that simple attitude was, and how it carried me through periods of the school day that were not obviously fascinating or easy. I also see how easy it is *not* to have that apprehension or expectation, to feel lost in a class, to feel stupid or incompetent, because I was pretty poor at team sports and my teachers and peers were not kind about it. Which meant I half-assed PE until I discovered track and field, and circuit training, where being gauche and myopic weren't such handicaps.

- **Sell the benefits.** Students often need to hear that if they behave in *this* way then they will obtain some other outcome they want, e.g. a grade, early break, a postcard home, a kind word, a job, entry to university, and so on. Being able to delay gratification and work, not for the activity itself, but for the result of the activity is one of life's gateway skills. More people like six-packs than like doing sit-ups. Keeping their eyes on the prize will motivate many students at least a little.

- **Do the right thing.** Some people are strongly motivated by values and ethical positions. Help them to understand why behaving like *this* is the moral, right thing to do. If you can persuade them that the behaviour you want is morally right, then you have a strong incentive for them to do so. Try reframing your request in a way that maps onto their existing moral values. For example, a student might be rude to you because they see you as being a hostile authority figure, but they may also value being kind to their peers, so if you explain that their behaviour hurts others' learning, you may be able to reach them that way.

3. COMPULSION – USE DISINCENTIVES TO APPLY PRESSURE TO BEHAVE WELL.

And sometimes students just have to behave whether they like it or not. This is not an uncommon situation and reflects a great deal of how the whole world beyond the classroom also works. Even law-abiding people often feel the desire to break a rule when it suits them, or when they feel they can get away with it, or when the benefit appears to outweigh the cost. And there are many people who are not normally law abiding and only follow rules when it suits them. The law is the law, and unless you have some unusual mitigation, breaking it will lead to consequences.

In schools, students have to abide by many norms and standards. Some of them are absolutely imperative (no knives), some of them are important (no shouting out) and some of them are desirable (walk sensibly to lessons). Some are even arbitrary, with no obvious benefit other than that they satisfy custom (e.g. having your top button done up). But if students cannot be persuaded to behave in the right way, every system, if it is to survive, reserves the right to compel. We see this in reasonably liberal societies all the time: it's better to drive carefully because you see the sense in it and value the behaviour. If you need some reminders, you'll find them in speed traps and sleeping policemen and road signs. And if that still doesn't work, you'll find yourself losing some points on your licence and facing a fine. And if that doesn't persuade you, you might find a judge impounding your car and a jailor tucking you in every night for a few months.

But a common consequence of some behaviour (e.g. speeding) is that, most of the time, there are no consequences. In an absence of consequences, it becomes more likely people will ignore rules, especially ones that seem arbitrary or unimportant.

Some commentators on education and behaviour seem to think all rules are upheld by compulsion or are the product of some tyrannical regime. In reality, compulsion is just the most visible tip of a vast iceberg of normative pressures on how we behave. Persuasion and indication are much more powerful (although less visible) levers. Many people *consent* to rules and routines because they value their outcomes.

I've listed ten principles of behaviour at the start of this book. Allow me the indulgence of suggesting an eleventh principle – a shadow principle:

We don't follow rules; we uphold them.

When we reframe our efforts to induce good behaviour like this, we can see that rules are not our masters; they are our moral compass. We don't obey them; we acknowledge their value. We recognise them. They are often underpinned with compulsion – because what is optional will never be universally adopted – but it is a mistake to assume that compulsion is the basis of all conformity to rules.

CHAPTER 2
WORKLOAD

Workload is one of the biggest challenges in the life of a teacher. So many teachers feel that they don't have enough time to do anything, let alone everything. The tasks you need to accomplish can expand to fit (and surpass) any time you possess. Your work is rarely, if ever, done. This leads to:

- Not doing everything, and running out of time to do important things.

- Doing everything, but badly. Half-arsing is the default coping mechanism of the chronically over-tasked.

- Giving up and clocking off. It's easy to lose heart and just stop trying or caring a little. This is another coping – or possibly survival – mechanism. You want to do your best, you want to succeed, but it's so hard that in order to stop breaking your heart every day, you stop caring a little bit. Sometimes a lot.

Workload isn't only a problem in teaching, and it has many roots. It is vital to realise you cannot do everything, even though the job will tempt you to try and the system is convinced that you can. This is often made worse by well-meaning but clumsy line managers who are themselves under the lash and on the rack of an impossible workload.

Managing behaviour well requires work before and after lessons. It is a process that is made possible by efficient admin. But this becomes impossible if the teacher's workload consumes the time they need to perform these vital tasks. So workload becomes the enemy of behaviour management. Detentions get missed; pastoral conversations never happen; planning for behaviour dissolves; the teacher starts to rely solely on their ability to maintain good behaviour as it happens in the lesson and following up vanishes. This spells doom for effective behaviour management.

New teachers, unable to gauge what the correct level of effort or output is, will often try to meet every demand asked of them. The system around them, frequently lacking in checks and balances, will – often unwittingly – expect them to do so. This is usually not a conscious decision by any one person, but many schools are not good at matching staff workload with staff capacity. Even experienced staff can be caught in this trap.

Taming the workload dragon

Needless to say, when workload is too high, nothing gets done well, things get missed, and corners get cut. None of these are ideal. Bad habits start to form, inconsistency is encouraged, and standards inevitably slip. There are many things in the school that the individual teacher has no direct control over. The only things you can directly control are your own actions. But there are some tactics that the individual can usefully employ in order to tame the workload dragon, if not actually slay it. None of them are rocket science, but I am constantly surprised by how often we forget to do these basic tasks:

- **Make a list.** The simplest time management device in the world. So simple you'd think everyone would use them. But they don't. It is easy to be swamped by the number of tasks that you need to achieve in education, in any normal day or week. Tasks for your classes, for parents, for the next week, for your department, for the parents' evening, and on and on. You can feel like you are drowning. Your brain isn't built to cope with holding so many things in your head, even if you are good at that kind of thing. Untamed, the multitude of tasks appears too big to possibly achieve.

  You will always suffer the niggling guilt that you have missed something important. There is only one way to beat this: write it down. Make a list. You think Santa remembers all those kids' names? As soon as you write down everything you need to do, you have named and tamed the things you fear. There they are, on the page, looking a bit smaller. More importantly, looking distinctly more *finite*. There aren't a million and one things. There are a dozen things, or two dozen, or ten dozen. The point is, they have a terminal point. Which means you can now…

- **Prioritise.** There are so many things that need to be achieved as a teacher. Some are must-dos. Some are would-love-to-dos, and some are would-like-to-dos. Some are orders, some are not. Not everything has to be done. Not everything can be done. This applies to all teacher tasks, not just behavioural ones.
  - ▷ Highlight the things that have to be done; the things that must be done (or the consequences will be unthinkable, career-ending).

▷ Highlight things that would be great to do.

▷ Highlight the things that – honestly – *don't* have to be done. Be brutal here.

▷ Make a side list of 'would-love-to-dos'.

- **Eat the elephant – one bite at a time.**[11] Allocate deadlines and time slots for the must-dos. You may be able to achieve something bit by bit. Or something may need a chunk of continuous time. Big jobs look as enormous and indigestible as an elephant. You can't swallow it in one sitting. But divide the elephant into smaller morsels and you'll find that – given enough time – you can indeed polish off what at first seemed impossible.

Knowing that a task must be done, but that it can be done on Wednesday, and you have scheduled this, is an enormous relief. Of course it means that you must stick to your schedule. Good advice is only as good as when it gets done.[12]

- **Rewrite deadlines**. Look honestly at your workload. Be brutally honest. With everything you have to achieve, can you realistically meet all your deadlines? If no, then approach the person who set them. Explain your current dilemma and ask if there is any flexibility. People are far more disposed to look well on someone who proactively manages their time commitments than someone who constantly fails to cash the cheques that their promises have written.[13]

- **Learn the power of a conditional yes.** People will bury you in tasks that they don't want to do but could do or should do. They may have the authority to direct you to do them. Whatever the situation, learn the *conditional yes*. This is not a *yes*. The temptation to just say yes to every job offered is huge.

But what takes someone a second to ask can take you hours or weeks to complete. I remember once being asked if I could 'just pick up a class to help out'. But 'just picking up a class' every week for two terms meant

---

11 Provenance uncertain. I found sources from Confucius to Archbishop Desmond Tutu. It was probably Marilyn Monroe.

12 Which sounds like something Forrest Gump's momma used to tell him.

13 Also solid advice for bank managers and loan sharks.

a time commitment (with marking and planning) of about 64 hours. 64 hours out of my waking, working life, in a sentence that took five seconds to say. Happily I was robust enough to refuse.

But I didn't say no. What I actually used was a *conditional yes*. I said. 'Sure, I can do that. What class can I drop to fit it into my time available to work?' I guarantee you the assigner has not considered this part. They will probably go back on their heels a little. But be serious, and don't be pushed aside. 'Of course I can do this, I'd be glad to. What do I drop?' You can't do everything. Don't act as if you can.

Note, this is also a conditional *no*, but calling it a *yes* makes it sound better for you.

- **Just say no.** If you don't have to do something, and you know your core activities will suffer because of it, say no. And don't feel guilty. Just say no. 'No. I could but then I wouldn't be able to do my job properly,' is the best answer in the world because it is true. That's no small thing to protect. If we were to do a few core things brilliantly, everything else would improve. But because we try to prioritise everything, nothing gets the attention it needs.

So work out what needs to be done, and do it, in a time-rational way. And reject or deflect everything else unless you are comfortable doing more.

Creating a calm, safe, dignified behaviour culture is *the* core task of running the room. From it, everything else flows. So it is essential that building behaviour is prioritised in the time you have available.

As Mark Twain once said, 'Buy land; they're not making it anymore.'[14] And like land, time is one of the most precious, finite commodities available to us. It cannot be wasted. I ought to say it *should* not be wasted because we can and do waste it, frequently. When we spend time on one thing, that is one token that may never be reused. But unless we master the time we have, we don't really

---

14   Also said by Lex Luthor in the 2006 film *Superman Returns*, echoing his earlier ambition in 1978's *Superman*: 'Stocks may rise and fall, utilities and transportation systems may collapse. People are no damn good, but they will always need land and they will pay through the nose to get it!' This, just before he decided to bin California and turn the Mojave Desert into the Marina del Lex.

spend it. We *leak* time. We throw it around like it's cheap when we think we have a lot, then try in vain to hoard it when we can feel it almost gone. We burn through it when we think it will never run out, until it does.

So time should be invested in culture planning, routines, norms, teaching and maintaining. And following up. And reminding students. And calling parents when you need to. And all the other things. But as much as possible, focusing on the admin that helps you to run the room is the kind of maintenance you need to invest in.

If someone asks you to help them put up some posters or run a club, do so only when you are sure you can complete everything else first. This is not just an essential thing to do if you want to do the job you want to do; it is also a good way to look after your mental health. You are – and remain – human. You should give your best, not your all, to the job. And your best is not possible when you give your all because you exhaust yourself. Manage your workload or your workload will manage you.

TEACH, DON'T TELL, BEHAVIOUR

Behaviour cannot be modified in the long term by simply telling students to behave. The behaviour curriculum must be taught, similarly to how we would teach an academic or practical subject.

CHAPTER 3
GETTING BETTER

In this book and in *Running the Room*, I have attempted to describe what some of the most effective teachers have done in order to create the best learning environment for their students. This book is not, by itself, a training programme, although it could easily be adapted into one.[15]

But many teachers, whether they are new or simply looking for a way to develop their existing skills, may need some ideas about how to improve. Learning anything is much more than simply reading a book, although reading a book can be part of that. Teaching and running a room is so much of a practical craft that it is essential for any practitioner to go beyond theory. You cannot learn to drive by just reading about it. Do.[16]

You can learn a lot about driving by reading theory; you can certainly learn the names of all the car parts, and where they should be, and what they should do, for example. And this will be a big help. You must learn the steps you take to start the car and set off. But you cannot learn how to change lanes, or overtake, or nudge confidently onto a busy roundabout by *only* reading about it. You can't learn to play in the Premier League no matter how many matches you've watched in the pub.

Training programmes within schools and institutions vary enormously in terms of quality. Some initial teacher education/prep is of such low quality that it seems to have been designed by evil demons whose aim is to make the job harder. And some programmes are good, and a few are great. And often, teachers will have to invest their own time and effort into their development. If your school or department is enlightened, they will be able to support you in these activities or be doing some of what I described already. I would encourage you to engage with others in your school to make this a programme of collaborative endeavour. Work with others if you can.

Here are some things that other teachers have found useful as a way to improve their skill at running the room.

---

15   Watch this space.
16   Or do not. What am I, your Jedi master?

1. Role play

This is a dream to some, a nightmare to others. Mileage varies a good deal. In some cultures, some people would rather saw their arm off with a cheese grater than do a role play. I would have included myself in this category, had I not seen how effective this can actually be. Find someone you trust not to mock you and devise a series of scenarios that you can act out (with yourself as the teacher, I should add). You will be amazed how easy it is to play the part of a belligerent child. Perhaps we all have it printed on our DNA – the language, the mannerisms, the stubbornness, the egotism. Like karaoke, once the initial awkwardness bump has been overcome, it is remarkable how quickly one can start to get into character. And what is more remarkable (and useful) is how strangely real it can feel to be placed in a social situation that one finds challenging. It can bring back, in a safe and controlled way, the feelings of inadequacy and anxiety one feels in a situation where you are seriously challenged.

The utility of this process is that you can try out things to say and things to do. You can work on your scripting. You can focus on your own reactions and emotional responses. Are there any bad habits you slide easily into, like sarcasm? How is that working out for you? After the role play, ask your partner what they felt about your performance. Ask them what you might have done. Ask how your responses were perceived.

If you want to take this up a notch, film yourself and watch back together. This has the obvious advantage of being able to digest the material at your own pace, and then review and return whenever you feel like it. But it can be done as easily without. You may even want to consider forming a trio, and – theatre style – play out your vignettes in front of an audience of one, who can direct and stop, pause, critique and advise. It may be more useful if that third party is an experienced room-runner.

The important thing is to try out new ways of thinking and acting. To develop habits in a completely safe space where the consequences of failure are zero. You want the lowest stakes environment possible. So, this cannot be part of your performance management cycle, or your staff evaluation process or anything else that attaches instrumental weight to doing well. This is your flight simulator. Crash as many times as you want. Crash better each time.

2. In-house coaching

One of the most valuable relationships a teacher can have is with an experienced existing member of staff who is not only good at running a room but also knowledgeable about how to instruct others in the craft. This aspect of education is frequently overlooked. However good we are at teaching students, the way we teach adults is often more patchy. Teachers are expected to just pick things up as they go along – a terrible model, of course. The art of explaining things well applies equally to instructing adults. The art of instructing others to instruct others is far, far too overlooked in the hierarchy of what we value.

And of course, if we want our students to learn how to behave well, we need people who can teach students how to behave – that is already a skill of some delicacy and scarcity. It follows that we need to focus on finding or creating a class of instructors who are capable of *instructing teachers to instruct students how to behave well.* You can start to see why this is not a common skill. There are more unicorns than such creatures.

But there is hope. In an ecosystem where these mythical beasts are not grown industrially, we are still fortunate that we can find them in the wild. In every school I have been in, there are staff who are fantastic at running their rooms, fields, and halls and who also understand what it is that they do *and* how to encourage others to do it. They may have had little formal training themselves, but they are articulate enough and wise enough to know when it is not happening and how to remedy it.

X-Teachers

These mutants are worth their weight in saffron. I have often found that, in many schools, they are massively undervalued. They may be vaguely appreciated for their quiet classes, their good results, their successful performances and so on, but you often see them discounted from school discussions on behaviour improvement. Sometimes this is because they lack official rank or status; sometimes it is because the people in charge of such things have tin ears for behaviour and prefer not to use their most effective staff. If you are weak at behaviour management yourself, it is a distressing and embarrassing truth to be reminded of this by someone formally inferior to you in the school system. Or, it may go against the ideological grain of the more senior person; they may feel that all students need is unconditional love, for example, which is of course only partly true, and therefore wrong.

Whatever the circumstance, *find these wise people.* Seek them out like rabbis or gurus and ask for their help. If you are lucky, the school knows who they are and has recognised them with formal rank. Sometimes they have not. But no one ever said you had to wait for a school to give you the trainer you need. Ask for their help. Ask your line manager to support this. There is no reason at all why the person formally and directly above you in the school structure should be good at behaviour management, because there is simply no mechanism in the process of promotion that guarantees this.

This relationship might resemble the padawan-master arrangement or senpai-kōhai. Or it can be more egalitarian. But whatever the basis, it should be collaborative and supportive. These things are not done *to* the learning teacher. The student grows in their relationship with the more experienced member of staff. They develop a common language, and develop expectations of one another that are healthy, predictable and always kind. The aim is always to get better.

The learning teacher should always be open to suggestions about how to improve. But it is not a one-way process. They should feel free to respond, to ask for clarity, to object, and to expect the trainer to defend their views.

3. Film your teaching

O wad some Pow'r the giftie gie us
To see oursels as ithers see us!

Robert Burns, 'To a Louse'

Few things are as edifying, or as difficult to endure, as watching oneself teach on film. It is much, much worse than hearing yourself speak on a voice message. But the value is enormous. In your mind, you have a picture of how you act and behave. Forget this. This is the picture you paint for yourself, and whether you flatter or flay yourself in your mind's eye, it will only ever be the shadow of the truth cast on the cave of your imagination.

See yourself, in the raw. You will see your verbal and physical tics and habits, including ones you never imagined. What you might have thought was enthusiasm may come across as obsessiveness; what you thought was energy may look like you need the bathroom.

You will notice when you let things slide. When you ignore some behaviours. The students you pick up on, and the ones you don't. You will see the behaviour that triggers you, and what that trigger looks like to others. You will grasp, painfully perhaps, how the class responds to your responses. You will understand far more deeply what you do that is effective and what you do that is not. You will see what you actually demand from children, as opposed to that which you imagine you demand.

Better still is if you can watch this painful process with your mentor or coach. They will help you focus on what is relevant and what is not. They will point out the behaviours you miss, your blind spots, and the beats or reactions that you ignore. They will be able to suggest differences you can make to your own behaviour and structures, and when to do so. They can suggest script changes. They can applaud when you do things well and help you to keep a very crucial sense of perspective on everything. If you want to learn, no one needs you to be overconfident or crushingly self-critical. Neither do you any good. The students don't need you self-immolating over your errors. They only need you to be better. 'Future you' needs 'present you' to learn. Everyone wins when you do. The only failure is to believe you cannot improve.

4. Plan structured (low-stake) observations

A similar effect can be derived from having your teaching observed. These sessions must also be zero-stakes. The teacher cannot be doubly crushed by the anxiety of knowing that their career rests on it. It should feel like entering a flight simulator, with the exception that the passengers are real.

The first observation should be a general one to determine the baseline and get a sense of how things stand. The mentor and trainee should have a discussion afterwards that includes both parties' views. The mentor should not come to the conversation with ready-made answers, but instead should interrogate the trainee to understand why they did what they did. Are they aware of what they did? Did they have a reason behind it? Was it effective? Did they notice? These are simple but powerful questions that can animate and inspire learning.

This initial meeting can form the basis of a programme of further observations. And it should be a programme. One does not learn to drive after one lesson. There needs to be a series of observations. There should also be clear outcomes and expectations for the process. Every observation should have a tight focus on a very few aspects.

Topics could include routines, entry, exiting, transition between activities, noise, settling the class, consistency, and so on. Try not to make it about everything all the time, or it becomes about nothing.

Suggestions should be made before and after the lessons. There should be a meeting to frame the next observation, and a debrief after each observation. This is quite a labour-intensive relationship if done properly. But it often cannot afford *not* to be done, and the opportunity cost of neglecting this aspect of one's practice is immeasurably greater than the investment in one's capacities which, if refined, generate enormous dividends for as long as one teaches.

The wise teacher recognises this investment as the best he or she will ever make. The wise school sees that it is the best way to retain staff, to maximise their effectiveness, and to build the best school with the resources one has. The wise sector knows that its health is composed of the flourishing of its constituent entities and institutions.

5. Listen to people who can do it

It is a truth universally acknowledged, that a single man in possession of an easy solution to classroom behaviour, must be in want of a classroom himself. This may not be *entirely* true, but there is the germ of a truth in it. Behaviour management has fallen out of favour for the last few decades. In this vacuum there has risen a strange priest class of people who believe they know something about it while having very little experience of actual children or classrooms themselves upon which to test the mettle of their ideas. In this odd community of rentagobs and armchair educationalists, we find:

- People who have never taught a lesson in their lives.

- People who have only ever taught in highly privileged circumstances.

- People who have only ever taught in one-on-one contexts, like tutors.

- People who have very strong ideological or political views about what human nature *should* be like.

- People who have managed to achieve rank and status in education without actually managing a hard class or challenging set of children *with success*. It is not enough to have merely worked in a tough school; although it is undoubtedly to one's advantage to have done so in the field of behavioural advice, it is still possible to have coped and endured rather than thrived or flourished in such environments.

This is not to say that people from these categories do not have the capacity to offer excellent advice to the teacher who wants to improve their behaviour management. There are armies of people who have expertise on these matters – psychologists, mentors, coaches and more – who have the wit to appreciate the broad range of evidence available, and the integrity to match their pronouncements to the evidence available to them.

But I frequently hear the most outlandish of behavioural advice given by people who have very strong views but little else. I would sooner take advice from the man who delivers my pizza.[17]

The safest thing I can advise is this: try to seek advice from people who themselves can demonstrably manage the behaviour of challenging classes. That's it. It's not the only group you listen to, but it's a healthy guide when managing one's own self-improvement. If such people give you an opinion, listen to it with gravity, but also interpret it in light of your own thoughts and experiences. Value it but scrutinise it. If the classes they run behave well *and* perform highly, it's likely they are doing something right. Many teachers can get a tough class quiet by giving them little work and lots of fun time-filling activities. But great teachers have higher standards.

If someone outside of this category offers you advice, accept it politely, but with the caveat of 'How do they know this? What is their angle? Have they matched their statements with the quality of evidence underpinning it?'

I once received some advice from an educational psychologist that a particularly difficult student didn't like to work for more than five minutes, so he recommended that in order to engage the student, I allow him to play on his phone every five minutes to rebalance his chakras or something. It wasn't even some kind of neurological necessity; the student just didn't like longer tasks. Given that this advice was impossible to follow while still running a classroom, I advised him that this was not a strategy I'd be following and we'd have to look at alternative ones. People with fantastic one-to-one expertise aren't always the best to advise on large group contexts, where multiple individual needs must be balanced. And vice versa, of course.

---

17   As an aside, the wisest piece of parenting advice I ever received was from a minicab driver in Glasgow. 'The most valuable thing you can give them is your time,' he said. 'That's what they want most.' I have never forgotten that.

I've been told that a student should be allowed to leave the room and go for a wander when they feel like it because it 'helps them stay focused'. What might be good for one student in a tutorial context could be devastatingly unhelpful in a classroom. Like it or not, we are where we are. Most of us will teach groups of students in rooms. That is the model we must optimise, not some idealised landscape where all students are the only students in the world, and we have infinite time to cater to their every whim or need. And not everything they want is a need. Some wants are just that – wants.

We teach classes, so we must get better at teaching classes. And to do so, we should listen foremost to those who have already done so, otherwise we platform and privilege the (no doubt well-intentioned) opinions of adults who think they're helping but cannot.

Only in teaching do we do this to ourselves. Let's not do it anymore. Let's recognise the extraordinary quality of experience we have within the sector, and platform and privilege that. That's how we propagate and multiply the very best of what we do, and build upon it, rather than stumble from generation to generation reinventing the wheel every few years and declaring it a breakthrough. And perhaps then – maybe – then we can call teaching a profession. I believe we can. But not yet.

6. Read, then practise

This is delicate. There are a great many books available that discuss behaviour. While all are undoubtedly well-meant, the quality varies from the peak of Mount Everest to the basement of the Mariana Trench. Some of this is because the authors have come from teaching backgrounds that lacked challenging students; some of it is simply magical thinking, and the hope that children are naturally good and kind and learning-focused. Some of it is ideological. Some of it comes from very scant experience of working with children. Some of it comes with simply focusing on one approach to the exclusion of others – for example, believing that *only* sanctions can improve behaviour or using *only* restorative approaches.

I argue that human behaviour and motivation are complex mechanisms, and to reduce them to a few simple levers is to court failure. If you want to motivate and direct behaviour as much as possible with as many as possible, it is vital to use as many different approaches intersecting with one another as you can.

Some students are motivated by the desire to please you, so acknowledge and encourage that. Some students struggle to imagine long-term outcomes, so assist them with short-term motivators like mild sanctions and rewards. Some students want to go to university. Some students don't want to disappoint their parents. Some children need to talk through their behaviour problems and need some pastoral support. Some students need to be told that they matter. Use all of these approaches and many more.

So be careful which books you choose to use in order to get better. At the end of this book, I've included a list of some texts to supplement this one. They have been chosen because they grasp what actual classrooms are like, appreciate the complexity of children's circumstances, and try to avoid simple ideological traps.

Reading can only take you so far. But it can be the beginning of a journey that leads to professional development. If they are read closely, and care is taken to consider what is meant and how it might apply to one's own circumstances, then good texts may light a fire that leads to action. If they are read critically and charitably, it can do some good. It can act as a spur to targeted self-development. It can lead, in other words, to a blend of thinking, acting and reflecting upon one's actions; and if this happens, then it might be useful.

But reading a book and doing nothing is a great way to donate money to publishers. If that's all you do, then just make sure it's not a bad book.[18]

7. Visit other classrooms

Seeing what others do, and what other classes are capable of, is one of the most powerful and refreshing experiences you can design for yourself. Teaching is frequently a lonely profession, which sounds absurd when you consider how much of a group project it is. But you can be alone in front of a crowd, and once the training wheels are removed, there is often a very strong sense of being solo with the children. Unless you are being observed, or you work with a teaching assistant or similar, it's lonely in the spotlight. After a few years, it's easy to forget that there are other ways to teach, to interact with students. *So get out there.*

Get out into the classroom next door. Get out into rooms where experienced teachers have their own styles. Get out into different subjects to learn what they do differently, and what they do the same, and what might be useful to you and your classroom. Observe with focus.

---

18   Feel free to buy this one again.

- What routines do they have in the classroom? What do students do without being asked? What cues does the teacher set to remind students?

- How do they respond to behaviour that is less than perfect? Is it effective?

- Look at specifics: entry and exit protocols, transitions between activities, questioning, answering, completion of work, and so on. What effect do they have?

- Language, tone, stance, volume, voice, movement, anything that subtly cues behaviour implicitly. How do students respond to it?

If you can, get into schools that have a similar demographic to your own but that also have greater impact, behaviour or standards. Ask what they do to achieve this. Above all, expand in your own mind the repertoire of what is possible. When visitors to extraordinary schools like Dixons Trinity or Michaela Community School leave, they walk away with a profound sense of possibility. They leave with a new understanding that what has always been is not what always *must* be. That understanding is at least as important as a set of new behaviour strategies, because before an action succeeds, it is an idea, and for the idea to escape the mind's laboratory it must be understood to be possible.

Teachers, I have found, need to see concrete examples to fully understand new strategies and behaviours. And why not? They are weary of Christmas cracker initiatives that are impractical, tiring and bureaucratic. If you want them to invest the tiny sliver of time they might have in changing anything, then they need to see it working, not just the theory. So, help yourself to understand, and go visit other schools.

This is not always easy – timetables are tight and dense, and who has time for idle pursuits? But it is a great investment. Speak to your line manager or training coordinator and ask if you can observe some lessons, and for your time to be protected then.

CHAPTER 4
YOU AND THE SCHOOL

Unless you tutor, or you run webinars for the sons and daughters of Swiss aristocrats, or you teach lone children who wander into your mountaintop Shaolin temple, you probably work in an institution – a school or a college. A lot of teachers come to this circumstance with very little thought for what that means, and often quite a few assumptions. I've seen many teachers who started their career fresh from university and knew only the education sector, or one school. So here are some of the things one should expect from working inside a school:

- A school is an institution. It is not a bunch of really friendly people who coincidentally meet up every day to do their jobs alongside each other. It is not a street market.

- A school works to budgets. Many of the decisions it makes are born of necessity or expediency rather than ideal practice. Teachers may not be qualified in the subjects they teach, for example. Or class sizes may be too great. Or a child may not have the support she needs with her SEN.

- Staff members are expected to conform to school rules and cultural norms.

- Schools are marbled by deep and extensive hierarchies that are not always easy to see. There will be vertical hierarchies based on status, but also hierarchies between departments, year groups, subjects, and even tenure, longevity, seniority, and personality. Status is accrued in lots of different ways. There are headteachers with less status than their deputies, and students with higher informal rank than some members of staff. A confident NQT can be more powerful than the unpopular head of a low-status subject.

- But most importantly, schools are webs of relationships. You are not alone, although some schools are run so poorly that you will feel that you are.

- You are responsible to multiple parties: to your own conscience, to your line managers, to society as a whole, to the headteacher, to the school, to the staff body, to the parents and to the students. You have many duties to all of these stakeholders. Understanding what your duties are is an important part of understanding what your role means. You do not simply walk into a room and teach. You are a teacher. It is much more than the verb. You are not just a human being who teaches.

Teachers are powerful collaboratively, but much less so alone. You must understand that being part of the staff body has rights as well as responsibilities, and advantages as well as restrictions. One of these is that you are not merely an atom, but part of a molecule. You are an organ in an organism; you are not a scrap of matter. When the body thrives, you thrive. When you thrive, the body thrives. Success is experienced mutually, and diffusely throughout the body of which you are part.

What this means is that when you succeed, your success is felt far beyond your personal domain, and others enjoy that success. But if you stumble, if you need help, there are others who should and must help you. You are part of a team, and when things are going well, that means a lot. It means that others will advise you and guide you; will share your burdens; will make allowances for you, or train you to do the role properly.

In practical terms, this means that others will remove children when they need to be removed, mentor them, train you, call parents, arrange meetings, cover lessons, park children, remind them of their duties and so on. You are not alone.

But you can make yourself alone. You can – as I did – cut yourself off from everyone, for fear of looking incompetent. You can neglect to ask for help even when you are drowning. You can be paralysed by the enormity of your problems so that you feel even to admit them would be a crushing admission of incompetence. You may fear for your job. You may wish to 'not look like a bad teacher'.

And the students will sense this. You may be able to hide your anxieties from other teachers or line managers with bluff, confidence and a poker face, but the children will not be fooled. They will know you never refer to other teachers or that misbehaviour is never recorded, that you never use the schools' systems, that no one is invited in to observe or support you. They will sense your alienation and dislocation from the school community. Some of the more vicious students will see a lone animal, struggling away from the pack, and sadly, some will respond by picking you off.

None of this needs to happen. You are a twig in a bundle. The bundle prevails, even if one twig breaks.[19]

So:

- Ask for help when you need it.

- Know the school behaviour policy.

- Understand the line management hierarchy intimately.

- Know who pastoral leads and heads are, form tutors etc.

- Use school data recording systems (see later).

- Ask for advice or help *before* you need it if you can, and when you need it if not.

- When you do need advice, ask for it, follow it, and make a record of what happened. Then report back to the advisor for further direction. This avoids advice sinking beneath the waves without trace, or bad advice being taken as a sign that the problem has been solved.

If you get into difficulty with behaviour:

- **Report** – record the incident.

- **Escalate** – if your in-class strategy doesn't work (e.g. if a student fails to report for detention, or misbehaves in a detention, or repeats the misbehaviour), *escalate the sanction* in exact accordance with the school policy. Record that you have done this.

- **Ask for help** – find out who needs to know about this escalation, inform them that you have done it, and ask for any advice at the same time as you are doing this. They may have good suggestions, or warnings to give, or background data that might be relevant, such

---

19   This sentiment is perfectly expressed in Aesop's Fable *The Old Man and his Sons*. An old man, near to death, teaches his sons about unity and strength by asking them to break a bundle of sticks. When they fail, he separates them and breaks them easily, one by one.

as the student's circumstances or some kind of parental or home information that might be vital.

Manage upwards

One of the most common issues new teachers have is a failure to be supported by line managers. Indeed, when I ran an online advice column for behaviour for the *TES*, it was probably the second-most-asked-about problem. There are lots of reasons for this.

Line managers are human too. If we prick them, do they not bleed?[20] You might be one yourself. Everyone is busy in schools – perhaps you've noticed. Everyone is walking miles and miles in their own shoes and may have multiple pressures on them to do many things simultaneously.

Which means they have limited time to do everything, including supporting people they manage, following up according to the school policy, and so on. If you set a sanction and the student doesn't turn up, and then the line manager fails to follow up, or attend a meeting with the student, we must remember that they are often as frail as us. This doesn't excuse any dereliction of duty, but understanding its root may help us to solve it.

How to train your dragon

Line managers may not be well trained themselves in school procedures or behaviour management. Training in this area is often very limited, and training for leadership roles is almost nonexistent. Many school leaders and managers are as self-taught as everyone else is in behaviour management. In this climate, it is more likely that they will often not be as rigorous as they should be.

Some line managers have very different ideas about what their role is. They may see their job in terms of dealing with curriculum, pedagogy, assessment etc., but may not see behaviour as their responsibility (beyond perhaps their own classes). Or they may think that behaviour is entirely the responsibility of senior staff.

The solution here is to try to influence your line managers to support you, or in other words *manage upwards*. It is a very hard thing to do for an individual teacher, especially if they are new, but it is often important. The key is to put pressure on the system to work better, and to help you. In some ways you are

---

20   Do not test this theory.

using the same techniques you would use to persuade a student, only this time on the colleagues who inhabit the same system as you.

1. Remind them persistently. Sometimes people just need reminders that they need to support you. Interpersonal skills are very useful here, as is *scripted language* to prevent misunderstandings.

    Example:

    'Can you remind me – are we meeting at 3 or 3:30 to discuss Ryan's behaviour with him?' Meaning: 'It's happening, and I'm reminding you but making it look like I'm asking for your guidance.'

2. If a breach of policy support has happened (for example, a line manager has failed to attend, or make a phone call home, or pass on some paperwork), then remind them of the need to do that in a way that doesn't grate.

    Example:

    'I know you couldn't make the meeting/didn't have time to write up the incident etc., but can you let me know when you might be able to do that? I know how busy you are, and I just want to plan around your schedule.' Meaning: 'Do it. Also, you are powerful and wise. Also, do it.'

3. If you feel they are seriously letting you down with their lack of support, put pressure on them by appealing to their finer instincts.

    Example:

    'I know you've been so busy recently, but I do need your help. Can we meet today so you can advise me what I should do regarding these meetings we couldn't have? Is there someone else you think I should be asking, as I don't want to put pressure on you?' Meaning: 'I am putting pressure on you and I'm not going to give up. In fact, I might ask other people to help me. How do you like THEM apples?'

4. Finally, you may have to be blunt.

Example:

'I'm really struggling here. The behaviour policy tells me to do X, but in reality X doesn't seem to be possible. What do we do? This is causing me real issues, and student behaviour is deteriorating as a result.' Meaning: 'You're killing me with this.'

At the same time, you may want to go sideways. In every institution there will be people who are senior to you, in experience or rank, who might be able to help you. Ask for their advice. They may be able to offer practical support as well, such as mediating a reintegration meeting, or speaking to a student, or their parents, or suggesting scripted language, or even how to manage the school system so that it helps you more.

A word about schools in general. If your school does not provide you with sufficient support to manage your classes' behaviour, or does not support you with the school behaviour policy by performing its started functions; if they advise you to get on with it alone; if they tell you you just have to put up with it; if they say, 'What do you expect from kids like these?'; if they tell you to sink or swim; if they focus on anything else other than creating a safe, calm learning environment; if there is no training to get better at behaviour management; if they don't know any more about managing behaviour than you do – if they do any of these things, then consider your position. There are better schools out there.

Who is responsible for behaviour in a school?

Everyone. But this obvious fact seems to come as a surprise to some. I commonly see two, equally wrong models:

Model one: schools that believe student behaviour should be almost entirely managed by classroom teachers alone. In this model, teachers are responsible for the behaviour in their classrooms. Which means that if students misbehave, teachers are almost fully responsible for doing something about it. Senior staff in this model frequently feel bothered by having to assist with behaviour, seeing it as a failure of the classroom teacher's ability, and therefore a failure of their leadership if they give in and assist them.

The classroom teacher is usually blamed when things go wrong. In this model, the duty of the leader is to make sure that all teachers know that their responsibility is to maintain order, by a combination of interpersonal skills and getting the students to like them.

This is usually done in the name of building relationships with the children. Leaders in these contexts are often unable to comprehend why teachers can't maintain order, while simultaneously themselves enjoying high status, lots of formal power, low or nonexistent timetables, or the best-behaved classes.

Model two: schools where the teachers (or even also the senior leaders) believe that behaviour is to be personally managed entirely by senior staff, like some kind of behaviour SAS. Even the smallest matter is delegated upwards. Whenever a student misbehaves, they are sent to the senior staff member's office, where justice is dispensed, frequently based on a chat and a biscuit. Teachers commonly feel that 'it's not my job to manage behaviour; I came here to teach,' or something similar. Children are often sent out for not having a pen. Senior staff are summoned to the classroom throughout the day, and exasperated staff say, 'Please sort *this* one out.' Teachers are free to teach exactly as they please, and pull students up for anything they wish, as frequently or as infrequently as they wish.

In my experience, model one is common. Model two is very rare. But we do see a lot of schools where staff think this is the model they want and behave on that basis. I go to a lot of schools where each group thinks the *other* group should be solely responsible. This is behavioural nimbyism – 'Not in my back yard.'

Both of these models have the same root: they both see behaviour as someone else's responsibility. And the root of this problem isn't normally laziness; it's *not knowing what to do*. It's a training issue. If people aren't trained to know how to run behaviour in a classroom, or as a leader, it's no wonder that the default model for many is 'Someone else should handle this.' For untrained leaders, it's 'the teachers'; and for untrained teachers, it's 'the grown-ups'.

But there is a better model that solves so many problems: behaviour is *everyone's* business.

Behaviour is everyone's responsibility

Film critics often talk about the role of the *auteur* in cinema. This means a director who has so much influence in every aspect of the film's creation that they could be classed as the author of the film itself, rather than merely an important part of an enormous project that involves the skills and artistic judgement of hundreds of people and moving parts. Hitchcock is often described in this way.

But the idea of the auteur has been criticised as over simplifying a process that cannot truly be described as having only one author. Films are collaborations. Even with the world's most gifted actors and directors and cinematographers, a dud can result. 'Nobody knows anything,' was a line made famous by William Goldman, referring to the uncertainty of a film's success despite it being built by the best talent available.[21]

There are no auteurs in schools. A school is an institution. It runs like an engine, the sum total of a thousand moving parts, as a collaborative project. People all have different roles. These roles are all directed to the mutual aims and goals of the school. When the school flourishes, the teacher flourishes, the student flourishes, the cleaner flourishes, the bursar flourishes. Even the flowers flourish. Different roles have different outcomes, but they lend themselves to greater outcomes and mutual success.

When the cleaner comes in on time, works well and diligently, then classrooms are hygienic and fragrant, equipment lasts longer, toilets remain in order, people can use the bathroom, etc. When the bursar succeeds, people are paid on time and bills get paid and books get balanced, and schools don't close. When a teacher works well, the students do well, the school's reputation is enhanced, other classes feel safer, parents don't think about moving neighbourhood, and so on. Take any one of these out of the equation entirely and see how long things last. Schools are like engines. Every part has a different purpose, but each part has a function in the machine. The engine grinds to a halt if you take one part away. Sometimes slowly, sometimes fast.

Here's a sobering thought experiment: how long would it take for your absence to become a problem? If you apply that to a school, what staff would you miss first? In my experience, the cleaners; they are the invisible but essential army of a building. Take them out and see how long life remains bearable, or sanitary.

So too with behaviour. Maintaining behaviour is not about small, discrete teams patrolling the corridors and classrooms and catching misbehaviour. Schools

---

21 'Nobody knows anything … Not one person in the entire motion picture field knows for a certainty what's going to work. Every time out it's a guess and, if you're lucky, an educated one.' Goldman, William, *Adventures in the Screen* Trade, Grand Central Publishing, 198. He could so easily have been talking about teaching. As Dylan Wiliam said so memorably, 'The rather terrifying thing about being involved in education at the present time is that we are the first generation of educators who know we have no idea what we are doing.'

are not panopticons. They are not turreted jail yards policed by wardens with CCTV and sniper rifles.[22] They are cultures. And cultures are an act of constant creation. They are built, maintained and reinforced. They do not last long if one person tries to build it by force, alone.

Behaviour is created by the community. Everyone in a culture is a member of that community; they are formed by it and they form it. They affect it and are affected by it. Nobody is separate from it. If a student sees an adult smoking in the school premises, or using their mobile phone in the corridor, and the rule is not to do either, then they will assume this is acceptable – for adults, or possibly everyone. It doesn't matter if it's the bursar or janitor. They are adults, and in a culture that is dominated by a hierarchy, that matters. All adults are role models for behaviour.

You are permanently on display in your school culture. You can never switch off. You constantly give off implicit signals about who you are, what you consider to be acceptable, and how you think it is acceptable to act in that culture. That in turn affects other people, and their perception of how to act in that culture. We affect one another. *No man is an island*, as John Donne said.

But everyone has a different part to play in that engine. In a successful school, the roles are well trained, explicitly understood, and systematically and consistently observed.

Example:

The school leader's role in behaviour is to create conditions where staff can do their jobs as efficiently as possible. This entails making sure:

- They are all properly trained to manage behaviour.

- There is a clear curriculum for social conduct.

- School culture is explicitly designed and reinforced.

---

22   At least I hope not.

The pastoral leader's role is to help make sure that teachers have a calm safe working environment where they can teach and where children have behavioural support. This might entail:

- Collecting children from classrooms when they misbehave.

- Monitoring student behavioural data to detect any worrying patterns.

- Liaising with parents to work out any support children need.

The classroom teacher's role is to create the optimal circumstances for students to learn, to be safe, and to be treated with dignity while doing so. This will involve:

- Knowing the curriculum.

- Planning lessons.

- Delivering lessons in a way compatible with the ability of the class.

- Setting clear routines.

- Upholding routines through consequences.

And so on. This sketch should serve to make one point: different roles entail different duties, which demand different training. If everyone performs their role well, everyone benefits. If someone neglects their role, or assumes their duties are someone else's, then the machine chokes.

Help me to help you

This is another reason why consistency matters. Every member of staff's behaviour has an impact on the working conditions for all other members of staff.

Example:

If one teacher sends children into corridors all day long as an off-the-record sanction, then other teachers' lessons are disturbed, and students learn to resent the school generally for treating them this way. Which is why training matters, to make sure that consistency is maximised.

It also underscores that there are many aspects of school culture that people will have equal or co-sharing responsibility to uphold. For example, it may be everyone's responsibility to hold doors open, or advise students which way to walk along a corridor, or maintain silence in assembly, and so on. Some members of staff may have greater responsibility to do these things; for example, a playground monitor may have the specific responsibility to intervene in the eventuality a fight breaks out, but there may still be some collateral responsibility of the bursar or the receptionist to do so if they saw the same thing.

Which is why it is vital that all staff are inducted into the school culture, from the admin staff to the pastoral team. Every adult and child is a member of the culture. The only question after that is, how will we train them to be healthy flourishing members of a flourishing community?

And the personal duties for the classroom teacher here are:

- Know the school policy.

- Don't work alone – use the school system.

- Always ask for help when you need it.

- Always offer help when you can do so.

- Uphold the policy whenever you can, and ask for help when you can't.

- Record as much information as you can without interfering with your primary functions.

- Don't assume someone else will pick something up.

- Always follow up with incidents.

- Manage upwards.

- Ask for training to do the role you have been hired to do.

This is how you manage to be part of a functioning team, rather than an island or a rogue element, undermining the greater culture. You are a professional, hired to do a professional role, which means being part of the system as much as possible rather than an observer to it. You are a participant and an important constituent of the school, not a ghost.

Warlords

Finally, while this book is aimed at teachers, it is important to acknowledge that building an effective classroom culture is *much* easier when the whole school culture is also based on clear routines and norms. This and similar considerations are beyond the scope of this book, as they fall more precisely under the remit of leaders and leadership.[23]

But it is worth mentioning it at this point: teachers by themselves can only do so much to create healthy cultures of behaviour in their classrooms. The principles I have outlined throughout this book are by far the best ways to get as far as possible towards an ideal classroom culture. But if the school culture is dysfunctional or chaotic, then even the best teacher will only be able to do so much. That may well still be a considerable amount – I have seen many brilliantly run classes in chaotic schools – but they will only ever succeed *despite* the school, when it should be *because* of it. They are warlords in a failed state; surviving but perhaps not thriving.

To summarise, and then move on: classroom teachers can create fantastic behaviour cultures, whatever the school environment. But if the environment surrounding the classroom is unsupportive, then it is ten times harder, and for some teachers it may prove impossible. This is not a judgement on the competency of the teacher, but a reflection of the difficulty facing them. Teachers can only devote energy to what they *can* do, not what they cannot. For teachers who wrestle with unsupportive schools, I can only offer one piece of advice: try to find a school that deserves you. That may not be possible, but collectively, teachers must strive to work in environments that sustain and encourage human growth, and put whatever pressure they can to persuade others to do so too.

---

23   See *Running the School: a leader's guide to behaviour*, John Catt Educational (2021)

CHAPTER 5
STARTING A CLASS

In narratives, few things are as important as the introduction. The first paragraph, the first chapter, are crucial. It can help determine if the book is brought home, downloaded, borrowed or stolen. It also foreshadows what to expect and prepares the audience for what is to follow.

Beginnings are important for teachers too. The two most important beginnings for teachers are:

- The start of every lesson

- But especially the start of the *very first* lesson

Research suggests that focusing on classroom management at the beginning of the class relationship is a critical ingredient of a well-run classroom.[24] Bearing in mind everything we already know about the importance of norms, routines and culture, we can now think about how your first encounter can successfully begin building these.

Before they eat you, they meet you

A good reputation is more valuable than money.

Publilius Syrus, Maxim 108[25]

Before you meet them, it is very possible the children have already met you. If you are an existing member of staff, your reputation will precede you, however unfairly. If the children are already at the school, they will have seen you. Their peers will have mentioned you. You may have some kind of formal role or presence in the school, or be a regular of the public areas. You may have some kind of online professional presence that the children and their families can access. They say you eat food twice: first with your eyes, then with your mouth.

---

24   Sanford, J. P., Evertson, C. M. (2012) 'Classroom Management in a Low SES Junior High: Three Case Studies', *Journal of Teacher Education*, v32 n1 pp. 34–38.

25   Syrus, P. (2012) *Sententiae*. Nabu Press.

The students meet you before they eat you.

They already have a sense of what to expect from you, even before you open your mouth to greet them. This is one reason why your name, your reputation (as in so many other aspects of life) is important. As a professional, you must always think, 'How do I come across?' I heard of one maths teacher who used to teach content right up to the very last minute of the last lesson of the last term of the year. Then, after summer break was over, the class would reconvene in his room, and the first words he spoke were, 'As I was saying…'.[26]

First impressions matter. Students are silently downloading data about you, instantly, constantly. I am frequently reminded of the conversation I heard once between two students in the school yard, which went like this:

'Have you seen the new teacher?'

'No, I wasn't in yesterday. **Is she strict?**' (My emphasis)

That speaks to me of a very deep and simple lens that children often have about teachers. There is a profound (albeit imperfect) difference between two major models of teacher-student relationship: do they (the teacher) allow you to do whatever *you* want, or do they insist that you do what *they* want? This isn't a moral judgement. I would advise that students need to know, very quickly indeed, that this room runs on rules. Your rules, of course.

Within seconds of seeing you, they start to make judgements about you, what you are like, and crucially what you will be like with them. Will they be able to proceed unfettered? Will you look after them? Will you make them work hard? Are you a 'real' teacher? None of this is fair. But it is going on whether you like it or not. So now is the time to work the hardest to make the right impression. Because any impression you make will form the basis of their perception of you and the sincerity of your instructions, and you will be struggling with or against these as you build your relationship.

Before they arrive

Get your room ready. Like cooking, you want to get as much prep done as possible. If you have your own room, then your work is much easier. If you are mobile, then you have to work five times as hard at this part. If you can, be there

---

26   Andrew Richards, Twitter, May 23rd 2018 www.bit.ly/374GcnK

early. This means five minutes at least. If you can't, you can't; but do whatever you can to make this happen.

- Check the room. Is it tidy and clean? Has the previous teacher left it in a fit state? If they have not, and they do this regularly, have a word with them. That isn't rude or pushy – it's a professional courtesy you should be able to expect and reciprocate. You need to build norms and boundaries with your colleagues too.

- Get all the equipment you need into the room for the lesson. Have *spare* paper, pens, pencils, books – whatever you need for your space.

- Have a tidy desk. Hide your personal items. Your neatness sets the bar for the class. If you are messy, why should they be otherwise?

- Dress for the part. Attend to your hygiene. I know that sounds obvious, but the number of teachers I encounter who think they can get away with skipping a shower suggests otherwise. Set a standard you want your students to aspire to. If you look[27] like you don't give a damn about your role, they will assume you mean it. Yes, it is perfectly possible to be the world's greatest, most inspirational teacher and dress like an unemployed wizard. But why make it harder for them to think you're serious about the job? Use every cue you can to suggest you're a professional. Never think that if you dress like they do at the weekends, they will think you are one of them. They will *never* think you are one of them, nor should you wish them to. If you are over 21 years old, they assume you go home and listen to The Beatles and smoke a pipe. Accept that what you are – what you aspire to be, what they need you to be – is an adult, and a professional. They don't need a tall chum. They need a teacher.

- Design a seating plan (see 'Seating plans', p. 145). This is worth a good deal of thought. Look at your room, and the furniture you have. What do you want or need? Change absolutely anything you want to make the room the shape you want, but don't be guided by whim. Ask yourself – will this aid learning? Will this help behaviour? As I discuss in 'Seating plans', the easiest and most useful default is probably a row/column design, which can then be adapted. If you

---

27   Or smell.

run a less grid-like space, like a science lab, or a machine shop, or a music room, or a drama class, then attempt to simplify the structure as much as possible. The default assumption that science must be done in groups, for example, should be challenged, especially when it comes to understanding the actual versus the perceived value of continuous practicals.[28]

Whatever you decide, make sure that the plan is where you want them to be. Look at any data you have available to you, especially if the student has a special educational need, some form of special circumstance, or a track record of poor behaviour. Usually the students who need the most support need to be kept closer to you.

As for your lesson plan, it should go without saying that the lessons should be designed in a structured way. Teachers sometimes feel they can fly by the seat of their pants, or they have observed others doing so and think they can emulate it. In reality, it takes enormous practice and knowledge to make a lesson that looks impromptu work. Simply turning up with a crazy idea isn't enough. Pedagogical and curriculum choices can have a huge impact on behaviour. Techniques such as direct instruction[29] or Rosenshine's 'Principles of Instruction'[30] are powerful tools to maximise student focus and engagement.

'Students will behave if you plan a brilliant lesson'

This was a commonly heard inanity when I was training. I still hear it, and it's still just as wrong now. If a student tells you to fuck off, it isn't because your starter wasn't clever enough. While it's important to teach the best lessons we can, the idea that somehow the structure and content of the activities are key factors in their behaviour is awful. It blames the teacher for behaviour that originates with the student. You know when the deputy head walks in and the kids all go quiet? How much planning did she put into that?

Instead, we should seek to grasp the kernel of truth amongst the weeds of the feelgood nonsense: a well-planned lesson *will help* behaviour, and a badly planned lesson makes bad behaviour *more likely*. But they are not the principle catalysts.

---

28   Boxer, A. (2016) *The Science of Science Practicals: Are We Wasting Our Time? Pt. 1*, A Chemical Orthodoxy, www.bit.ly/3pZRUsq Retrieved 22/01/2019

29   www.amzn.to/33g1LjV

30   www.bit.ly/2Ja0pAA

Scripting your own behaviour – the most important homework you will ever do

In advance of your first encounter with students, you need, in your own head, to be absolutely certain about:

- What your behaviour expectations actually are.

- What standards you will accept.

- How you will teach them.

- What you will do if they struggle with the expectations.

No teacher should walk into their classroom without considering these aspects in great detail. They are the core function of an educator. Get this aspect of your role right, and everything else gets easier. Get it wrong, and everything else is ten times harder. It is of great consequence for a new teacher (or a teacher new to a class) to make this investment. And it is an investment – one that pays enormous dividends. It is hard work. But fighting the same pointless battles your entire career is, I assure you, far harder.

HOW DO YOU DO THIS?

A good teacher training programme should devote considerable time to developing the beginning teacher's behaviour skills. If it does not (one can only wonder what could be of greater utility), then the teacher must develop this aspect independently.

- Read extensively about behaviour.[31] Sadly, some texts are hopelessly impractical, ideological or too distracted by how they would *like* children to be rather than how they actually are. Very few of them are of much use to anyone with an even averagely challenging class. If you come across one of these texts, then to quote Hume, 'Commit it then to the flames: for it can contain nothing but sophistry and illusion.'[32]

  Instead, focus on material that leans heavily towards basic psychology and practical experience of working with challenging children in

---

31 For instance, try *Running the Room* (2020), Bennett, T.

32 Metaphorically, of course. Only Nazis burn books. Hume, D. (1777) *An Enquiry Concerning Human Understanding*. London: A. Millar.

a mainstream classroom context. Try to avoid leaden 19th-century philosophy that speculates about the nobility of the natural child, or 20th-century dilettantes who desperately want children to be the vehicles of a revolution they themselves will never endure, taste or pay for.[33]

- Reflect upon what you believe desirable behaviour to be. Take time to consider it. Ask yourself what you *really* mean by good conduct; what kinds of behaviours you expect to see, and why you expect to see them. Ask yourself what children will need to do in order to thrive in your classroom and consider in detail the micro behaviours that follow these answers.

  Feel free at this point to drill down as deeply as you please. This is where you start to realise that a lot of what we expect them to do is quite hard if you're not used to doing it, even simple things like lining up, sitting properly at a desk and so on.

- Turn these behaviours into a list. Think about what good and bad executions of these would look like. Ask yourself what behaviours are the most important, and how you will communicate that to the students.

- Devise a lesson plan (or a series of lessons) based on teaching these behaviours. The minute you start to think about behaviour as a curriculum is the minute you start to understand how to improve behaviour. 'Getting them to behave' isn't a battle of wills, or a few dramatic moments of misbehaviour and response. It's a programme of study. And you, I believe, are the teacher.

This is all *before* you meet them. Hard work, to be sure, but necessary, as the architect's plans are to the builder.

The first physical encounter

In the first encounter, you are not trying to achieve perfection. The gardener doesn't expect flowers an hour after sowing the seed. First meetings are for planting, for foundations. You will build upon this in every encounter you have with the students thereafter.

This is important because teachers often expect things to be perfect from the beginning and, with such an impossibly high aspiration, feel a failure when this

---

33   For a good selection, see 'Further reading' at the end of this book.

does *not* happen. But imagine the absurdity of a doctor beating themselves up because patients aren't cured by one spoonful of medicine. Expect things to be imperfect, without ever accepting that they must always remain so.

The honeymoon effect

There is a common experience amongst teachers who take over a new class, where they encounter reasonably good behaviour for the first few days or hours and start to think that all will be well. 'This isn't so hard,' they tell themselves. 'I was told these kids were a challenge!'[34] But this is a classic example of the *honeymoon effect*, when teachers and students exist in a fluid state, where the children are not sure of the new teacher's expectations and may themselves be working out where they stand in the social web of the classroom. Children can often be cautious while they work out where your boundaries are. This can lead to a false sense of calm.

The danger is that the teacher can be encouraged to take their foot off the pedal a little; to ease off on their boundaries. *These children are all lovely and agreeable*, they think. *Perhaps I don't need to lay down my expectations quite so firmly and clearly. Let's just get on with some great learning!*[35]

Build a ceiling before it rains

Gather ye rosebuds while ye may,
Old Time is still a-flying;
And this same flower that smiles today
Tomorrow will be dying.

Robert Herrick, 'To the Virgins, to Make Much of Time'

'All shall be well, and all shall be well, and all manner of thing shall be well,'[36] said Julian of Norwich, the 14th century mystic. But she never had to deal with wet play in a primary school. To simply wait for things to go wrong is a mistake. Fix things when they are not broken. Build a ceiling *before* it rains. Make hay *while* the sun shines. If things are going well, and if students are being biddable and peaceful, use that calm space as an opportunity to lay down the boundaries and set the expectations they need to flourish. Don't waste that precious time

---

34 Often they go home feeling like Michelle Pfeiffer in *Dangerous Minds*. The week after, they feel like Saint Sebastian.

35 Reality makes mincemeat of such Polyannas.

36 Julian of Norwich (1901) *Revelations of Divine Love*. Methuen

loafing. You will pay a thousand times for blowing this chance. Honeymoons are lovely things, but don't push your luck. Trusting that all will be well is a great way of guaranteeing that your luck will run out, fast.

Lay your stall out

This is the time to tell them who you are, who they are going to be, and what the rules of the room are. This is the time to be clear, to be confident, to be precise, and to be ambitious. Beginnings are for beginning, and subsequent layers have to be built on solid ground. So, what should your foundations be?

Teach them that:

- The classroom is a learning space.

- You have high expectations for them.

- What they do matters to you.

- Everyone in the class is part of a community.

- The community succeeds together.

- This success is achieved through a set of behaviours.

- You will teach them these behaviours.

A script to begin a class

It is impossible to be completely prescriptive about this. The school will (I hope) have some procedures already in place. Your local circumstances will dictate some of the specifics. But here is a suggestion:

Example: secondary school

- Students are asked to line up outside the classroom. The teacher directs them into the kind of line they want, explaining what that means.

- Students are directed into the classroom and asked to be quiet as they do so.

- They are directed to stand and wait at the back of the class.

- Once everyone is at the back, the teacher addresses the class with a very short welcome speech:

'Welcome to my classroom. My name is Mr Bennett and I look forward to teaching you this year. Before we begin, we need to find our seats, so when you hear your name called, take your seat quickly and quietly. Remove your jacket, place your bag on the floor, place your planner on the desk, face up, and read the sheet on your desk until we're all ready. Thank you.'

The teacher then directs students to allocated seats. Once done, names are checked against planners to make sure everyone has succeeded in finding their seat.

'Thank you for taking your seats quickly, we've got a lot of learning to do and I'm looking forward to starting with you.'

The teacher then directs students to be quiet, waiting for complete focus before proceeding.

'Thank you. Welcome to class X, my name is Mr Bennett, and this year we'll be studying Y. It's a subject I love to teach, and it's one I hope you will find interesting too. I very much enjoy teaching it to students like you, and I know that every single one of you can succeed, no matter well how you've done before. I'll do my absolute best to try to help everyone succeed.

'I want everyone to be safe here, to enjoy the lessons, and to do really well. But you can't succeed unless you also try your hardest. In order for us to all succeed, we need to follow some simple rules. Let's go through them now.'

The teacher then runs through all of the basic classroom rules with the students. Not only does this involve explaining what they are, but also explaining why they are important.

Example:

'It's important for us all to be on time, because that means we can all start together, and no one misses anything. It also means that we don't have to waste time waiting for people to catch up because they were late. So, we all make it a big focus to be punctual. That means we walk straight from the last lesson to this one with no diversions or hanging about. You get to the classroom within two minutes of the previous lesson's bell. If you're any later than that, I'll need to mark you late and you stay behind at the end of the day for ten minutes with me. If the teacher before kept you for any reason, they have to give you a note to excuse you. No note, you get a late mark. If you're late for a good reason and you have no note, you still get a late mark, but you come see me after and I'll make a judgement. But it has to be a very good reason, like you helped carry someone to see the nurse. Anything less, and it's a late mark. If we're all punctual, we show respect for everyone else, we show respect for our learning, and it's good manners. Being late when you don't need to be tells other people that you matter more than them. So, in this class we show compassion and respect for others by being on time for them. And me.'

Understanding is checked. This might take the form of verbal questioning, asking students to repeat back instructions, a group discussion about when the rules might be hard to follow, what we can do to make them easier etc. A multiple-choice quiz, a short essay, or any other form of informal assessment if it supports the learning.

After checking understanding, the teacher might want to get the students to practise the habits and routines expected. For example, if you want them to understand how to line up, get them to line up. If you want them to understand getting ready in the line-up, tell them what you'll be looking for, then look for it.

Challenge it when it's not there yet. If you want them to go straight into lessons, then send them out, explain what they have to do, then ask them to do it. Correct any mistakes, or better still send them out again to perform it again. If you want them to understand the basics of getting ready at their desk, then explain, and get them to do it, over and over a few times if you need to.

Explain how you would like them to start and finish their work in their books. Put an example on the board, then ask them to do the same in their books. Get them to hold their books up to see if they managed it. Get them to do it again. Explain how they should ask and answer questions. Hands up? No hands up? Flash cards? Get them to demonstrate what they have learned from you, and celebrate success when it happens.

Go through homework routines: how to do it, what it involves, how long it should take, what isn't an acceptable piece of homework, what happens if it's late, how to make that better, and the consequences of being late. Tell them how to avoid it.

Tell them how you want them to sit, if you have a preference, *and* how you don't want them to sit. Most importantly, teach (not just tell) them what *good* behaviour is, not just bad. Tell them of any reward strategies and prizes you employ, as well as any sanction systems you use. Express the strong hope that you won't need to use sanctions but that you will if you have to. Explain why.

> 'Everyone here needs to help everyone else by following the rules. If you can't, I'll help you. If you don't understand them, I'll tell you. If you need help, it's there for you. But if you choose to ignore the rules, then you have to get a sanction. This is to help you remember not to do it next time. I'd much prefer it if I never had to set any sanctions. Instead, I'd love it if I was always proud of you.'

Throughout all of this, constantly mention that you have high hopes for them, you want them to be safe, and that if everyone behaves kindly, like a good student, then everyone will do well and enjoy lessons a lot more. Explain that you won't tolerate anyone feeling unsafe, or abused, or threatened. Explain that you care about their wellbeing as well as their education, and *that's* why you're so strict, or you have such high expectations.

Teach them what silence means, what quiet work means, and what an acceptable level of talk is in a talking task. Teach them what can be discussed and what can't, and what will happen to them if they do.

> 'When we speak to the rest of the class, e.g. when answering a question, this is the volume I want you to use. [Teacher demonstrates it.] Everyone hear that? I'll do it again. Now Ryan – you show me that volume please. When was the Battle of Hastings? [Ryan answers.] Correct. Now, Jasmine, was that volume right? Show me what you think it should have sounded like. Ryan, try that again. When was the Battle of Hastings? Much better.'

Teach them how you will indicate that people need to be silent. Teach them what listening looks and sounds like, and the message you will give to get it. Teach them how long it should take to get it.

At the end of the first session

Set a piece of homework – something simple, but indicative of how well they can follow an instruction, what their admin or memory skills are like and so on. You can tell a lot about a class from who responds. My personal favourite used to be a behaviour contract, stuck in their books, which they had to get their parents or guardians to sign – that was all. Most students could do it, but some would forget etc., which gives you an immediate sense of who is organised, compliant, etc.

You can dig into the non-compliance a little – maybe there's a home situation to contend with, for example. But the point is, you have learned something, and they have learned something. And don't let anyone off with non-compliance – it needs a bulletproof excuse or they receive a sanction or some form of consequence. No casual exceptions. Teach them that you meant what you said, right from the start.

Then explain how you will dismiss them at the end of the lesson, and how they should prepare to leave. As with any whole-class direction, wait for complete silence when you prepare to dismiss them, and expect that silence to be maintained throughout. Then dismiss them the way you said you would. If they don't do it properly, hold them back until they do. If any misbehaviour has been intentionally disruptive, then set a sanction; if any behaviour has been unintentionally disruptive, then have an immediate post-class conversation about it – if time permits. If it does not, find a time.

Then shut the door, and record anything that needs to be followed up with later: exceptional or exemplary work that needs to be congratulated in some way; misbehaviour that needs to be recorded on the school system or conveyed to line management or pastoral teams. Record exact insults, verbatim. Record briefly any misunderstandings that arose, or anything that needs to be corrected in the next lesson, or anything that needs to be practised. Record what hasn't been taught or, most importantly, learned.

The Curse of the Black Dot

And try to remember what Bill Rogers used to describe as the 'black dot in the white square'.[37] Imagine a black dot in a much larger white square. The black dot represents the misbehaviour that occurred; the white square represents absolutely everything else that happened. Many teachers find it very hard not to focus on the black dot, and overestimate the amount of poor behaviour there was, because their attention is drawn to it. But this may bear little resemblance to the reality of the room. Worse, a teacher can beat themselves up over the dot,

---

37 Rogers, B. (1993) '"Black dot, white square": Managing Stress'. A paper delivered to the 1993 conference *Student Behaviour Problems: Positive Initiatives and New Frontiers*. Evans, D., Myhill, M. and Izard, J. Camberwell, Victoria: ACER Press.

and forget all the great things that were happening. Remembering the black dot can stop you going mad. New, tough classes will take ten years off your lifespan and turn your hair grey if you let them. So try to focus on the positive as much as you can. In most lessons, a lot of kids are doing a lot of what you ask them.

Consider how the behaviour outcomes achieved in that lesson met the expectations of the behaviour syllabus you wanted to teach them and plan your next lesson accordingly. At the same time, think about blending the curricular content into the lesson.

Example 2: PE lesson

As above, but with the following emphases:

- Teach the correct equipment they need to bring; teach them warming up exercises; teach them about health and hygiene; teach them appropriate levels of contact, and how to play safe; teach them about uniform requirement; teach them game rules, explicitly, and with the understanding that what is obvious to the sporty child may be apocrypha and obscure to the less active one.[38]

- Teach them what effort looks like physically, and how to maintain it. Teach them how to stop instantly and pay attention to the teacher. Teach them exactly what they should be doing at that moment. Commonly PE teachers will employ a whistle, a bell or a specific verbal signal to achieve this, often because they are teaching across a distance, and listening is harder in the middle of a physical effort. Some classroom teachers also employ cues, whether a whistle, tapped glass, a hand in the air, and do on. It doesn't matter. What matters is that these things are understood by the teacher, clearly taught, and understood by the students.

Example 3: reception class

- Self-registering; finding one's hook, and where to put equipment; games and play tasks to settle children in; bathroom requests and dealing with accidents; where to sit on a carpet; how to transition between spaces in

---

38 I remember with horror being expected to play cricket (in Scotland!) one day early on in my secondary school. I'd never heard of such a thing, and I stood dumbly at what I later learned was a wicket, hacking away at fast balls like an executioner at his business as an audience of better-informed donkeys brayed at me. Excruciating.

the classroom – e.g. carpet to table, table to carpet, and teach them how fast you want that done.

- Teach them the procedures for asking for help; teach them what you expect them to be able to do to get dressed, and what to do if they need help. Kind hands, kind mouths...

The younger the child, the greater the probability that they haven't been shown or trained (or they are unable) to behave ideally. Junior school teachers or those teaching infants are often far more aware of (and therefore better at) this explicit phase of behavioural instruction. The same principles apply: clarity of expectations; avoiding assumptions that they know or can do things. Remember how scary and confusing classrooms look and sound to someone who isn't good at navigating them or doesn't understand the rules of the room.

Tease out misconceptions; demonstrate what you mean *a lot*. Check for understanding. Say things as simply as possible but no simpler. Say as little as possible, if that.[39] And repeat things about a hundred times more.

Consequences are still very important to the younger child, but remember that the intended effect of sanctions (to deter) will be far less effective with young children. One main reason for this is that very young children simply lack the kind of associative imagination to usefully connect behaviour with incentives and disincentives in the same way as an older child. Their capacity to inductively infer from their circumstances is still developing. Using such strategies as a thinking step may still have utility, as long as it is followed up with a good deal of explanation, unpacking and so on.

Remember: you cannot simply punish someone into being good, and that principle applies far more to children the younger they are. That doesn't mean you avoid using sanctions, but they must be used very differently, and with a different emphasis, than with older children.

Other contexts will require different routines and norms. Music lessons need explicit instruction on how to obtain, use, handle, play, maintain and store instruments; where to place them when the teacher is talking; what appropriate volumes might sound like; the penalties for misuse and so on.

---

39   'I'm not gonna say any more than I have to, if that.' Chili Palmer, *Get Shorty* (1995)

Drama lessons are sometimes hard to get right, because students are often permitted far greater physical and verbal licence than in e.g. a maths lesson. But I have also seen some immaculate drama lessons because the teacher has explicitly defined the boundaries of good and bad behaviour. One thing that many effective drama teachers employ is a clear and clearly taught signal to gather the students' attention from a lively talking task. So decide what the students should do at this signal, and how quickly. This is the equivalent of the PE teacher's whistle. Martin Robinson, author of *Trivium*,[40] describes this as teaching them to appreciate and execute a threshold moment, a transition from one state to the next.

How long do I spend on this phase?

As long as you need to. Some teachers will spend their whole first day going over the behaviour in this phase. In secondary, it should at least form most of the first lesson. But even after the first day of lessons, it should be built upon in subsequent lessons. Remember, it is a syllabus, and it takes time to unpack and practise and embed. Some schools, like the Michaela Community School in Wembley, London, devote an *entire week* to this phase, so never feel that you have to hurry up. Working hard on your foundations leads to a more stable building.

Recap

Golden rules of a first encounter:

- Think about social behaviour.

- Think about learning behaviour.

- Use a substantial part of your first interaction purely for direction on social and learning conduct, classroom values, and why we behave the way we do.

- Design lesson activities that exemplify how they should work.

- Temporarily sacrifice academic syllabus content for clarity of behavioural instruction and practise.

---

40 Robinson, M. (2013) *Trivium 21c: Preparing young people for the future with lessons from the past.* Crown House Publishing.

MAKE IT EASY TO BEHAVE AND HARD NOT TO.

Some students find it harder to behave than others. Remove any obstacle you can to them developing better habits. Provide support for them to achieve the expectations you have of them. Challenge low standards every time. Make good behaviour satisfying.

CHAPTER 6
LOW-LEVEL DISRUPTION

Low-level disruption is high-impact. It's not 'low-level' at all. It's serious, because it's by far the most common form of misbehaviour. What makes it so pernicious that so many teachers treat it as chaff; acceptable losses in the quest to get to the lunch bell. But it's kryptonite for lessons.

The best way to deal with low-level disruption is with the principles and systems I advocated in *Running the Room:* setting norms and routines; clear, high expectations, monitored and reinforced; reminders, warnings, support, consequences and constant reboots of the standards. All of these will minimise low-level disruption. The more it's deterred, the less chance it has of becoming the norm, which means you see it less and less frequently. And crucially, the more you focus on the small things, the less chance there is of such things escalating into bigger, more grievous misbehaviours.

Sweat the small stuff

Nip early, nip deep, never ignore if you can. Teachers should respond to misbehaviour when it is still a sapling rather having to chop down the trunk.[41] It expends less energy in its correction. Don't delude yourself into hoping it will go away if you ignore it. This is no time for misplaced optimism. Small fires become big fires, needing ever escalating responses. Tackle fires while they are small (and of course, better still, make your classroom fireproof).

Routines and rehearsed responses remain your go-to tactics. When students know how to behave, know that they are expected to behave, know why it is important, know it is normal, *and* know that there will be consequences for not doing it, then it is far, far more likely that they will do the small things better. I say 'small things' but nothing is truly small. A brick is small, but walls are made of such things, and palaces made from walls. Good behaviour is a big idea, made up of thousands of little behaviours that must be learned and practised and maintained.

What you accept becomes acceptable

This is why you must never say, 'I don't sweat the small stuff, I'll only intervene seriously when bigger misbehaviours happen.' By then it's too late. By setting your

---

41   Pharaoh had the same idea in Exodus.

bar of intervention so high, you tacitly suggest to the students that anything short of extreme misbehaviour is basically OK, or at least not offensive. Which normalises the lower level misbehaviour and invisibly encourages it! Remember Lemov's maxim: *What you permit, you promote.* Or mine: *What you accept becomes acceptable.*

Can I ignore any misbehaviour?

But can we ever ignore some misbehaviour? What about ignoring some misbehaviour in order not to provoke more misbehaviour? That sounds reasonable, but it is a thin end to a very dangerous wedge.

Example:

Kieran has just tumbled in late to your lesson,[42] huffing and capering as he does so. But Kieran is often absent, and often late. It feels like a minor miracle just for him to be present and equipped with a pen. So you turn a blind eye.

As you start the first task, he shouts out a few times, but you ignore it, because you want him to settle in. But he doesn't settle, instead asking everyone else for a pen. So you give him a pen rather than say anything about equipment. He doesn't have a book, so you don't say anything, and hand him some paper. He keeps making animal noises when everyone else is being quiet. You ask him to stop it, but nicely, because you know he responds badly to challenge. By the end of the first task, you've managed to explain less than you wanted because you had to keep attending to him. You look at his work and find there isn't any, but an impressive phallus drawn with an arrow next to it that says, 'Teacher'. You ask him to do some work. He tells you the lesson is boring. You smile and say, 'Bored is boring! If you try it, you might like it!' He throws his head back and snores loudly like a sailor.

And so on.

You see what is happening? In a noble but misguided attempt to encourage him into the fold, you've broken every standard in the book to make it as easy as possible for him to join in. You may even see it as a reasonable accommodation. But what is the net effect? None. Nothing he did was met with challenge. He was permitted to act exactly as he pleased. He knew that a sanction wouldn't follow. Everything he wanted to do, he got to do. He did nothing and learned nothing.

---

42   Imagine!

The rest of the class had their learning ruined. Worse, perhaps, is that you have sent a message out to everyone in the lesson: 'It's OK to act like this. I won't do anything about it. I'm just pleased to see you here.' This normalises it. Some of the least well-behaved children will be thinking, 'Why shouldn't I act like this too?' next time they feel like it. You just took away one more reason for them not to misbehave.

Ignoring misbehaviour is very, very often a very, very bad thing to do. In the scenario above, it would have been far better to:

- Immediately remind him of what he had to do.

- Check if he understood the task.

- Praise him for coming in, remind him he is welcome, and you will help him.

- But nudge him into realising that there's work to be done and other people matter.

- Get in there with verbal warnings and nonverbal, subtle cues so that he has as much chance to get on task as possible.

- Deflect: ask him what he understands or ask him a question.

- Distract: say a few brief words about something unrelated.

- Ask him what question he's up to.

- Quietly help unpack the task.

This is time consuming, but far more effective than pleading or ignoring with no consequence. There is no flesh to that strategy; no aim, no process or theory of change. It's just wait-and-see and cross-your-fingers. Good luck with that.

And finally, if he persists in his chaotic path, start to gently, quietly apply consequences, and finally remove him if necessary to a prearranged space. Because while Kieran matters, so does everyone else in the room. If you sacrifice their learning in the hope that it will appease Kieran, then what does that say about your attitude to the class? Every child matters.

The Land of do-as-you-please

'Let's dig an enormous castle!' cried Moon-Face. 'Then we can all sit on the top of it when the sea comes in.'

'We can't,' said Silky, suddenly looking sad.

'Why not? Why not?' cried Joe in surprise. 'Isn't this The Land of Do-As-You-Please?'

'Yes,' said Silky. 'But it's time we went back to the Faraway Tree. This land will be on the move – and nice as it is, we don't want to live here forever.'

'Gracious no,' said Joe. 'Our mother and father couldn't possibly do without us.'[43]

It is important that the student in this example and the rest of class realise that the class is a sacred space, a special place where people are safe, where things are calm, where learning is celebrated, and so is effort, kindness and a hundred other things. But it is not a youth centre. It is a room buzzing with purpose. It is not a place for students to decide if they will try or not. It is not the *Land of do-as-you-please*. When everyone is free to follow their desires, fewer people achieve anything important. What seems appealing at first must be tempered with the certain knowledge that most of what we truly value in life is achieved by effort, self-restraint and patience.

The classroom is a place where people try, where they are cared for, and where sometimes that means they are challenged to be more than creatures of desire and reflexes. That's true compassion: when we show people better paths and better habits, rather than a fraudulent, synthetic version of happiness, where we allow everyone to avoid even a moment or a morsel of dissatisfaction.

Our job is not to make them happy. It is not our role to please them or to avoid disappointing them. Our role is to be an adult and a teacher. They *need* us to be these things, even if at times they struggle to grasp why. We are not there to be liked, but to do what is good.

And ironically, when we do, they often like us more, and they are usually happier too. Who knew?

---

43   Blyton, E. and Hargreaves, G. (1981) *The Magic Faraway Tree.* London: Dean.

So, can we ever ignore bad behaviour? Yes, but always purposefully. This is called *tactically ignoring* misbehaviour – it is not simply ignoring it. It is done to serve a greater end. It is done with a sense that it *will* be dealt with at some later point in another way, just not *immediately*.

Example:

You are giving instructions to a whole class. You see a student texting under the table. You are in full flow and you have the full attention of every student. You know the student is volatile and responds to challenge with melodrama. You decide to tactically ignore the isolated misbehaviour because it is not disturbing others at this point. You finish your instructions.

Meanwhile, the phone has been put away. When you have finished instructing the class, and everyone has begun, you ask the student to accompany you outside, with their bag, if that is where the phone has gone. You confiscate in the corridor, where fallout can be minimised. Or you wait until the end of the lesson, as long as you remember – and you must remember.

This is an option. I would still recommend in most circumstances you respond at the time, in order to reinforce the bond between action and consequence. But tactically ignoring has its uses, and it is an act of judgement to know when to employ it. It is a utilitarian consideration, always done for the greater good. Remember, you have a whole class that relies on you, and is relying on you to maintain as much flow, and therefore focus, as possible.

Ignoring by design and time management

Teachers frequently spend most of their time responding helplessly to poor behaviour. I call this **cart and horse** or **marionette teaching**: the pupil pulls the strings and the teacher dances. You often see this in classrooms where the students are highly resistant to direction, and the teacher is oversensitive in their response to student misdemeanours.

People tend to respond more to anything that indicates threat, alarm, or danger. **Negativity bias** or the **negativity effect** is a well-observed phenomenon where unpleasant or threatening events or ideas provide a bigger draw to our attention than neutral or positive events.[44] This may even be an evolved trait that aided

---

44   Fiske, S. T. (1980) 'Attention and weight in person perception: The impact of negative and extreme behavior', *Journal of Personality and Social Psychology* 38 (6) pp. 889–906.

our survival. The gazelles that live to breed and pass on their genes are the ones who assumed every ripple in the pond is a crocodile. Confident, optimistic, happy-go-lucky gazelles end up as snacks.

This is why the news is full of disaster and drama, rather than charming stories about successfully risen loaves of sourdough, however well-proven they are. Imminent danger gets our attention, understandably. But this lens, so useful as a general principle when a car rushes towards you while a lovely balloon simultaneously sails across the pavement, can also lead us to *over*focus on the intense and threatening.

When we teach, we will never achieve perfect behaviour from all. There will inevitably be small acts of disturbance. But this is a feature, not a bug, of human behaviour. The teacher should rightly be drawn to misbehaviour in order to correct it, but also be cautious not to completely focus on it. This is because some students know that teachers can be distracted, or annoyed, or agitated in some way by mucking around. And if they know that their behaviour will trigger a strong reaction from you, then some will do so for amusement, show off to their friends, avoid working, feel important, and so on.

Experienced teachers learn to choose not to focus on negative events, until they need or want to. Inexperienced teachers find their concentration sucked into turmoil without realising it. Teachers who want to move from the latter to the former start thinking about what matters, and how to prioritise their limited resources of attention, effort and time.

Takeaway: make it easy for students to learn by NOT behaving in a way that disrupts the lesson.

Cutting the strings

The way to avoid this is by being hyperconscious of your own reactions, and by avoiding snap judgements, emotional decision making, and outbursts driven by anxiety. Instead, manage your own behaviour. That's easy to spell and say, hard to do. Here are some practical tips to achieving this:

- Script your responses as much as possible.

- Have key phrases ready to say when you need to respond to misbehaviour.

- Have a plan for removal for when you need it. This will reassure you that you have options if things don't go well, which will reduce your anxiety.

- Clearly remind students of rules instead of blurting out the wrong thing.

- Only respond when *you* are ready, not necessarily immediately, unless there is an urgent need to respond instantly (for example, an imminent threat to a student, a serious misbehaviour like racism or violence, swearing etc.).

- Respond when you have time. You are not superhuman. Deal with things when you can, because you have to keep the lesson flowing. Make a judgement call about what is more important: responding to this behaviour or a greater aim.

    Example:

    You are working with an individual student on something they are really struggling with, but another student across the class is shouting and laughing. The student you are with is very anxious and hasn't been in lessons for a while. You only have a few minutes until you have to dismiss the class.

    1. You could stop what you are doing with the child who needs you and reprimand the other student, check what they're doing, redirect their focus, ask them if they need help. But this is a zero-sum game. You have robbed Peter to pay Ryan. The first student has lost out and the second has gained that most finite of resources, your attention and time. And that may well be exactly what they wanted in the first place.

    2. Or maybe you need to tackle it right away; maybe it's too disturbing to allow. In that case, do what you have to do, but make time somewhere else for the first student, or you teach the class that misbehaving is the way to get your attention. Or maybe they just give up because why bother? Think about the signals you give off to all students, not just some of them.

    3. Or you can make a different call, stay with the first student, and redirect the second from across the class.

    4. Or chose to tactically ignore their behaviour if (and only if) it isn't causing too much disruption, and you weigh up that

student 1 will benefit more than the loss overall. Then follow up with the second student later.

Avoid emotional outbursts. It may feel like the right thing to do, but it is almost never the *actual* right thing to do. It is also precisely what some children want. You become, in the absence of television, their television. You are the show. Come see the teacher flake out; marvel at the fireworks, as you sit and do nothing but gawp and laugh.

Don't be that person. Lead, don't follow. It's very easy to get caught up with the moment, instead of deciding what you really want and carrying it out.

Example:

A student says loudly, 'Fuck this lesson,' so everyone can hear. You ask them to wait outside. Instead of doing so, they start a loud, animated conversation about how they're being stared at by some students across the room, how they don't understand the work, how you haven't explained it properly, and five other things.

The danger is that you start having a conversation with the student about these things. Meanwhile, the whole class has downed pens and is watching with curiosity, boredom, delight, at the theatre unfolding before them. Learning has stopped for 30 people.

▷ Stick to the plan. You asked them to leave. Ignore their banter. It's chaff. It's strategic. It's a diversion.

▷ Ask them to leave again, calmly, more pointedly perhaps.

▷ Let them know what will happen if they don't leave.

▷ Tell them what is going to happen. This isn't a negotiation. You're informing them.

▷ Stick to your guns. They have to leave, especially if they've sworn loudly. Don't back down, and don't let it slide if they agree to calm down. All you do is teach them that if they break the rules, and argue with you a bit, you'll let them off with it. You encourage them to do so again. You encourage others to do so when they too feel like it. It's no different to the parent who says 'No' to a child asking for a biscuit at bedtime, but after ten minutes of gales and shouting, gives in…and feels like they did really well to hold out for ten minutes. The point being that the child now knows that enough howling will change your mind. The battle was lost, not won. It wasn't even a Pyrrhic victory.

Consistent compassion

Stick to your guns. Mean what you say. Always do what you say you will do. Always follow up. This is the true definition of *strict*. For some, this word connotes disproportionate levels of punishment and authoritarianism. But it simply means sincerity. It means carrying out what you said you would, and doing so reliably, regularly. It is *compassion, demonstrated consistently*. (More on compassionate consistency in chapter 9.) It is the glue that holds everything together. Consistency without compassion is unjust. Compassion without consistency becomes indulgence. Blended together, they become the philosopher's stone of behaviour management. And when you plan your own behaviour like this, you see it as a series of strategic responses rather than simply acts of desperation born in the moment of threat.

Summary:

- *The most effective teachers prevented poor behaviour as much as possible – they 'set the tone'.*

- *Respond when you are ready.*

- *Lead, don't follow.*

- *Don't be the puppet teacher.*

- *Deal with incidents when you have the capacity to do so.*

- *Demonstrate high levels of self-control.*

NO ONE STRATEGY WILL WORK EQUALLY WITH ALL STUDENTS.

You cannot punish students into behaving. You cannot reward students into good behaviour. You cannot tell, teach, trick, or nudge all students into better behaviour habits. Different people are motivated for different reasons. The wise teacher uses a range of strategies to reach as many students as possible.

CHAPTER 7
EFFORT

Sloth makes all things difficult, but industry all easy; and he that riseth late must trot all day, and shall scarce overtake his business at night; while laziness travels so slowly, that poverty soon overtakes him.

Benjamin Franklin[45]

It is strange how attitudes to laziness have changed in a few decades. Once, if a student didn't produce an expected amount of work, or put sufficient effort in, it was assumed to be the responsibility of the student. The fault lay with them, and the name given to this vice was laziness. Fast forward, and we frequently see a lack of output as a symptom of some factor external to the student – poor teaching, uninspiring delivery, inappropriate content, the wrong curriculum, topics that aren't 'relevant to their lives' and so on.

I once taught a boy who was bright enough – literate, reasonably read – but who was terribly lazy in my lessons. Because of his maths grades, he was registered with the school as 'gifted', although UK teachers may understand how mercurial this term can become. He was above average. But his output in my class was so low that one parents' evening I thought it important to mention this. I would frequently have to remind him not to lie on his hands and try to fall asleep. His work was scrappy, and bare minimum didn't begin to describe it.

But when I mentioned this to his mother, a prosperous hedge-fund manager, she turned the tables around and started to reprimand me. *Why weren't my lessons inspiring him? He finds the work too easy. I should give him more challenging tasks.* I explained to her that I couldn't give him more challenging work because he hadn't demonstrated that he'd picked up the basics of the material. His carelessness meant he barely took anything in. I told her that there was no point moving him to harder material until he could show me that he understood the foundation material.

But oddest of all was the suggestion that *he should only try in subjects he was interested enough in.* What one person finds enthralling is another's Ambien.

---

45   From his chaise longue, probably.

It was also sobering to consider she believed lessons were only worth bothering with if they constantly thrilled the class. Sadly, adults who role-model values like that help to generate student behaviour that disables rather than enables children.

At least they're quiet

Some teachers don't see laziness as misbehaviour. In fact, if a teacher has struggled with seriously challenging classes, or students, then it can be quite a relief to discover students who are merely lazy, quiet and unresponsive. *That's one less body to worry about,* to some extent, and you can focus on the pirates. But a moment's reflection will teach us that this attitude won't do. Laziness, low output and low effort *are* misbehaviour. How could it be otherwise?

It's important to redefine misbehaviour as 'anything that impedes learning or diminishes the dignity of others' and move away from a simple understanding of it as 'swearing and fighting etc.'. Because then we can see that laziness is as much 'bad behaviour' as many more obvious forms of challenging behaviour.

And it's a serious misbehaviour, because it leads to less learning. It's voluntary quarantine inside a lesson. It's a temporary exclusion, only within the classroom rather than without. It is possible to be present on the register but absent in the lesson. It is bunking, mentally. It is virtual truancy. It has the same effect. So we need to take it seriously.

There are lots of ways to address insufficient effort:

- The best, most important tactic is to teach students to understand what an acceptable level of effort is, and crucially what an *unacceptable* level is too. More than this, enthuse students with why hard work in general is valuable – exciting, even. Make it clear that they will be expected to do their best, *minimum*, not because they should be scared not to, but because it is just what people should do in your room. It will take some time to make this normal. But setting it out clearly from the beginning, with examples, delivered sincerely, and challenged when it fails to happen, and celebrated when it does, will help to build the norm.

- With every task, give students some kind of indication of what you expect them to achieve, and by when. This will help them plan their task time and aspire towards completion rather than assuming (often correctly) that a half-assed effort culminating in a half-arsed dash for the finishing line, will be accepted. Because this is really the clincher: you get what you expect. You get what you allow. If you allow students to turn in half-arsed pieces of work without comment, then you encourage them to do so again. You have made it easier for them to misbehave.

Make it hard to be lazy

- Make it hard for them to be lazy. Every time a student fails to reach the effort target you decide, challenge them on it. By far the easiest way to do this is to make them redo the work to your satisfaction outside of lessons. They will probably huff and howl, but do this two or three times and even the most slothful of students will realise it's easier to do it in the lesson than not.

- If students say they don't understand the work as an excuse not to have done it, then make sure your pedagogy nails clear explanation, with checks built in to establish if anyone needs directions re-explained etc. As with any strategy, this will not work with all students all of the time, but it will work with most students most of the time.

It is, in many ways, a win/win. You either identify a learning need or topic that needs to be retaught, or you get a student to redo their work and complete it. It's laborious, but the investment of time is worth it if you can habituate a student into putting more effort into all of their subsequent work. As with any such sanction/reinforcement, it must be consistent. If they think they'll get away with it sometimes, then they will be encouraged to try not to do it every time.

- A word of caution: when students redo work, make it easy for them to do so. Give them clear instructions about what you expect to see. If you allow them to simply half-arse work again, and you throw it back at them, you'll only antagonise the student.

Of course, it's still *their* responsibility not to be lazy, but always ask yourself, how can I make it easier for everyone to win here? Or do I want to deliberately make it easier to wind the student up? That's rhetorical, obviously. Don't accept one-word answers or a minimum effort twice. Demand full sentences, fully rounded thoughts, and make it a condition of completion. And when they redo work properly, thank them, explain why you asked them to do it like that and express the hope that you'll not have to ask them again. As with any restorative conversation, paint a picture of what better behaviour would look like.

And if the new work is improved, make sure you congratulate them. They need to see the positive benefits to doing well. And the next time you see them, remind them gently that you want to see the fantastic effort they managed to demonstrate the last time you spoke. Prime them to recall what real effort actually means in your lesson.

CHAPTER 8
FOCUS

How long can you focus on something? It seems to depend on a lot of things. If something is important, or if the consequences of not focusing are very negative, we can find focus easily. A gun pointed at your head does wonders for your motivation. If you enjoy something, that helps. If you're curious about something, that helps too. There are so many factors that affect focus. Difficulty is one. So is the object's perceived importance to us. Another factor is 'being used to focusing'. Focusing is hard. Focusing on something you find hard (and therefore not immediately pleasant) is harder still.

If you find some/all of your students struggling to focus then make it easier for them to do so. Focusing is a habit as much as an intentional decision. When you say to a room of children, we will all now read silently for 20 minutes, that may be 20 minutes longer than they are used to reading. So build it up like a habit.

- Describe exactly what you want them to do.

- Start reasonably small – a five-minute reading?

- Build the habit up by repetition.

- Then build upon the habit by extending the demand – five minutes becomes ten, and so on.

- Then repeat.

Focus becomes easier when it becomes habitual

Remove all unnecessary distractions. This is yet another of the many benefits of a calm, quiet classroom. I frequently hear the view that a busy classroom can be chatty and useful. And of course, conversations can be purposeful and effective. But noise by itself is not an aid to learning; it is undoubtedly a drawback to most, if not all, students. It represents a stimulus that leaches away the precious real estate of the student's attention, which is finite in quality and quantity. If they are attending to one thing, they are attending less to another. Noise, even noise that fades into the background, still distracts, and voices distract most of all. So, the most important distraction to be removed is the chatter of voices in disharmonious and unfocused cacophony.

What other distractions can we find?

- Busy walls, heavy with well-meant but ultimately useless recommendations and information.

- Other students. Classroom arrangements that emphasise being in contact with one another – grouped tables, horseshoes etc., may serve other purposes, but they do undoubtedly act as a clear incentive to focus on peer groups with their infinite attractions. See 'Seating plans, p. 90'.

- Bees.

Cognitive load theory

This theory has fast become a rich seam for educators.[46] Developed by John Sweller, it addresses the fact that people have limited bandwidth to process information from the outside, and that in order to do so most effectively, the amount coming in at one time must be streamlined, limited and orderly. If we present students with a text to read (e.g. on a powerpoint) while simultaneously speaking to them using different words, then we are asking their brains to do two things at once: read and listen. These are different processes; the text content is different and requires different focuses. It is much harder to comprehend two texts at once. Or to be more accurate, you can, if you accept the trade-off of massively reduced comprehension for both. Multitasking as we commonly understand it is a myth. It's really task-switching, which has high costs in terms of comprehension, focus, retention etc.[47]

The takeaway for teachers is that if you want students to focus, make it easy to do so by making sure you do not overload the bandwidth of their comprehension. This is achieved by:

- Presenting material in one medium at a time or presenting it in a multimedia way that actually aids comprehension rather than swamps it.

---

46 Sweller, J., van Merriënboer, J. J. G. and Paas, F. (2019) 'Cognitive Architecture and Instructional Design: 20 Years Later', *Educ Psychol Rev* 31, pp. 261–292.

47 Kirschner, P. and Bruyckere, P. de (2017) 'The myths of the digital native and the multitasker', *Teaching and Teacher Education* 67.

- Presenting new material in a simple way, giving learners more direct instruction and unpacking basic ideas if they are new to the topic, followed by practice, then feedback.

- Only moving on to more complex material when learners are secure in their understanding of the foundational concepts, language and material.

Behaviour management and pedagogy are inextricable; how you teach will affect your ability to direct the behaviour in the classroom, and your ability to direct the behaviour in the classroom will affect your ability to teach. This book and its source *Running the Room* focus on the behavioural aspects of this equation, but in truth there is much overlap. It is probably possible to be a terrible teacher in terms of pedagogy – you may drone on for ages, explaining little or repeatedly sending children to the textbook for endless, repetitive work – but still have very focused and attentive behaviour because of your ability to create and maintain norms. But no one would claim this was ideal. Not only that: a scenario like this guarantees that you will find it much harder to help students reach their potential.

Not everything is fascinating

Never try to improve student focus by vainly trying to make everything fascinating. This is unicorn hunting. You will never achieve it. This does not mean try to be boring. It simply acknowledges that nothing is universally gripping. Everyone has different interests. Your task, should you choose to accept it, is to help students learn about things that may appeal as well as those which may not. But you want them to learn the sweet fruit of learning and know the taste of success. You want them to know what it means to win a thousand tiny victories every day by grasping something, remembering something new, making new connections, and gaining a broader and deeper understanding of the world, themselves and their place in it.

Surprised by satisfaction

Our aim is to help them find *satisfaction* in learning, which doesn't always mean joy, or pleasure, although both can be found on the way. *That* is the best way to build up focus, because then the student chooses to learn, looking forward to what they will discover on the adventure. That is when students really see the value of the subject for itself. They see the intrinsic value in what they are doing, rather than believing that by doing it they will achieve some other goal, like a grade, or a job.

But instrumental ends aren't unimportant for focus either. Learning because it forms part of your broader goal, to achieve a good grade, to qualify for a college, even to make your family proud – these are still valuable things. And sometimes our motivations can turn on a dime. As a school student, I was dutiful and driven. I worked hard because it was what one did, and I didn't question it. And I enjoyed it. But then I left school a year early to attend university at 16, only to realise that electrical engineering was not my life's ambition after all. I dropped out after two days and returned to school to lick my wounds and grow up a little. But when I rejoined the school year (late, of course) all my ambition for classwork had withered, and I trod water for the rest of the year, something I had never done before. I had lost the habit, and I had lost my way a little. Motivation is the fuel that fires us, and without it, you aren't going anywhere.[48]

Motivation and focus are best developed through a magazine approach – use as many strategies as you can:

- Teach as well as you can to encourage students to be as enthused about the topic as you are. Lean on sound pedagogy like Rosenshine's 'Principles of Instruction',[49] for example.

- But also tell them the instrumental benefits of getting a good grade in the subject.

- We also want them to have a strong relationship of trust and respect with the teacher, so they work hard for *you*, and achieve for *you* as an adult role model.

- Also make them realise that effort below a certain point will not be tolerated, and you'll use consequences to gently nudge them back onto the table.

These are all different approaches. Why pick just one? Use them all. People are complex, and teaching is hard. You need every arrow you've got in your quiver to get through it and get through to them.

---

48   Which is probably why I ended up in the lucrative, live-fast-die-young-leave-a-beautiful-corpse world of university philosophy.

49   Rosenshine, B. (2012) 'Principles Of Instruction: Research-Based Strategies That All Teachers Should Know', *American Educator* 36 (1) [online] Available at: www.bit. ly/2Ja0pAA [Accessed 1 December 2020].

CHAPTER 9

WHY SO SERIOUS? HUMOUR AND THE TEACHER PERSONA

I can smile, and murder while I smile.

Gloucester, *Henry VI, Part 3*, Act III, Scene 2

You may have heard the old maxim, 'Don't smile until Christmas.' Of course, it's an absurd piece of advice to take literally. There's nothing wrong with smiling. After all, why do we smile? It's an interesting topic. We seem to smile for many reasons. When it's connected to sincere laughing, it's often involuntary. When it's done consciously to others, it, like all communication, is subjective.[50] Sometimes we smile to convey comfort; sometimes, friendliness; sometimes to show we're happy, and so on. Old Gloucester, above, even does it to conceal bloody intent.

Don't smile until they graduate

Dr Harry Witchel says, 'According to some researchers, a genuine smile reflects the inner state of cheerfulness or amusement. However, behavioural ecology theory suggests that all smiles are tools used in social interactions; it claims that cheerfulness is neither necessary nor sufficient for smiling. Our study showed that in these human-computer interaction experiments, smiling is not driven by happiness; it is associated with subjective engagement, which acts like a social fuel for smiling.'[51]

So smiling means lots of things. What is important is that children see you as an authority figure *and* as someone who cares about their wellbeing – personally and educationally. Those two roles complement each other.

---

50   Witchel, H. J. et al. (2018) 'A trigger-substrate model for smiling during an automated formative quiz: engagement is the substrate, not frustration', *Proceedings of the 36th European Conference on Cognitive Ergonomics*, Article No. 24.

51   *Smiling doesn't always mean you're happy*, news article on University of Brighton website, www.bit.ly/3qeHBkh, retrieved 10/03/20

Wire mother and cloth mother[52]

These terms originate from the work of American primatologist Harry Harlow, who designed an experiment to see if baby monkeys would form stronger attachments with an artificial 'mother' made of wire but who provided food, or a soft one made of cloth that was comfortable to touch and had no food. The results were clear. Not only would frightened baby monkeys often choose the comforting cloth mother, but 'they would open a door, hour after hour just to see [the] cloth mother through a small window'.[53]

This rather heartbreaking study for me suggests (rather than demonstrates) that teachers must be seen as having an interest in their students' outcomes and general wellbeing. If they think you are nothing but an authority figure who doesn't care about them, you may achieve compliance, but you will never inspire the greatest of effort, dedication or independence of learning. Students may behave better when you are there, but when you are not, they will decide their own behaviour.[54]

On the other hand if they see you *only* as a source of succour and compassion, then they may like you a good deal, but they will resent any attempt by you to make them learn anything, or indeed do anything they don't feel inclined to do.

Both roles must be learned and developed together, like vines growing together in a double helix. There is a third option that blends these approaches and draws on the best of them both: Mary Poppins.

The Mary Poppins teacher

We must never take fictional teachers too seriously, given that they don't teach real children, their results are unavailable for inspection, and they don't actually exist. When I hear someone tell me they were inspired by *Dead Poets Society* and want to be like Robin Williams's showboating progressive teacher John Keating, I think, 'What, unemployed, and in disgrace?' All fictional teachers can do is offer us metaphors.

---

52 Harlow, H. F. (1958) 'The Nature of Love', *American Psychologist* 13, pp. 673–685.

53 Hawley, P. H. (2018) 'Three Lessons From Wire Mother', *Psychology Today*, 23rd June. www.bit.ly/3mt5PVE

54 I had a teacher in secondary school who covered our biology lessons on a long-term temporary basis. Memorably, he told us, out of the blue and for no reason, that he hated teaching, he had no interest in our results, and he couldn't wait to get a real job. My God, we would have crawled through a minefield for that man. Or not.

And metaphorically, Mary Poppins[55] demonstrates a useful combination of qualities: a sincere desire to keep children safe, to nurture and inspire them (the spoonfuls of sugar), married to an implacable, indomitable will ('spit-spot!'). An adult who cares, but cares enough to challenge young people to be better, to try harder, even when they can't see why at the time. Lemov[56] popularised the *warm/strict* idea of teaching, and I think this neatly encapsulates this approach, which I call *compassionate consistency*. Each side of the equation must be embodied by your tone, style and approach to the students.

Compassionate consistency

Research also supports this compassionate/consistent approach. One study[57] identifies two crucial planes in the student/teacher relationship: *dominance vs submission*, and *cooperation vs opposition*. Reassuringly, high *dominance* simply means clarity of purpose and strong guidance, both academic and behavioural. High *cooperation* means high levels of concern for the needs of others and working as a team rather than just as an individual. Low cooperation means to be antagonistic towards the students, or even vindictive. But high dominance by itself can lead to lack of attentiveness to and concern for student needs and interests.

The evidence shows that in order for a teacher to have the optimal relationship with their classes, they need to have high – but not too high – levels of dominance and cooperation. This entails lots of clarity, purpose and guidance, as well as lots of concern for the interests of the students. In other words, the *Mary Poppins teacher*, compassionately consistent and practically perfect in every way.

An adult who is too jokey, too pally, too jovial, can be seen purely as a nurturer, not an authority figure, or worse, inconsequential and unserious. If children don't know you well, then if you're lucky they may think that you are nice, but they don't have to listen to you. When teachers begin their careers, they frequently err towards the side of cooperation, and over time (sometimes years) work out how to get better at being dominant.[58]

---

55   The film version, less so the book. In the book, she was often self-absorbed and capricious.

56   Lemov, D. (2010) *Teach like a champion: 49 techniques that put students on the path to college*. San Francisco: Jossey-Bass.

57   Wubbels, T. and Brekelmans, M. (2005) 'Two decades of research on teacher–student relationships in class', *International Journal of Educational Research*, 43 (2005) 6–24.

58   Wubbels, T., Créton, H., Levy, J. and Hooymayers, H. (1993) 'The model for interpersonal teacher behavior' in Wubbels, T. and Levy, J. (eds) *Do you know what you look like? Interpersonal relationships in education*. Falmer Press/Taylor & Francis.

But they need to see both in you. 'I care, and because I care I'll direct your behaviour, so you flourish.'

So where does that leave humour?

A smile by itself can mean many different things if accompanied by other behavioural context cues. The Batman's Joker may be a clown, but his smile is terrifying because it creates a sense of the uncanny when combined with his murderous and psychopathic intent. Or a frown can be funny, if delivered by a miserabilist comedian like Jack Dee or Denis Leary.

Many children, especially younger children or those with speech and language difficulties or autism, find sarcasm very hard to spot and process correctly. They frequently take irony literally, which can lead to some distressing and confusing misinterpretations of what you meant. Telling a child with a completely literal schema that 'You'll kill them if they're late again,' would be an extreme and obvious mistake. But even milder forms of this can be problematic. 'Here comes Mr Slow Coach,' might seem the gentlest of rebukes, but if the student doesn't have a strong relationship with you, if there is not already that bond of trust and mutual expectation, then it can be perceived as an insult. It *is* an insult, but when it's given to someone we know very well, they usually appreciate that it's been said in a knowing, friendly way. But if the student is hypersensitive to criticism or used to being mocked at home, they may see your light gag as a threat, and respond accordingly. In other words, be very, very cautious about using humour.

Given that behaviour is complex, 'Be cautious how much you smile' is probably the germ of truth at the heart of the command to park your grin until Hanukkah. You *can* still smile. Just remember:

- Don't assume you all share the same sense of humour.[59]

- Curb your enthusiasm for complex and extended gags.

- Avoid big, public jokes where the punchline is a student.

- They need to see you as an authority figure who cares, first and foremost.

---

59 I once knew a teacher who would 'treat' his class for good work by showing them 'things he found amusing on the internet'. The class would sit, stony faced, as he burned hours of their time on obscure sitcoms that he liked and they hated, which they told me. 'But we don't want to hurt his feelings by telling him,' they said.

- Let your humour come out in drips, once you are confident they won't misinterpret or exploit it.

- Don't frighten them off with hyperjoviality.[60]

Once you have built up a relationship with your class, where they trust you to say what you mean and mean what you say, you can test out that relationship, and even develop it with more generous helpings of humour if that is your bag. So they can see you smile at any time you want, but be sure that you work on your routines and norms and expectations at the same time. Then, you can smile as much as you like.

Humour is the outcome, not the process

In 2011, Channel 4 in the UK screened *Educating Essex*, a hugely successful fly-on-the-wall fixed-rig documentary series filmed in an English comprehensive school. At the time, the more conservative sector of the popular press made much of a clip where an English teacher dismissed his class of year 10 boys by saying to them as they left, 'Clear off, scumbags.' Imagine saying such a thing to children! And normally I would completely agree. You should never use such language with most classes.

But the reality was that the teacher in question was a brilliant professional with an enormously strong relationship with every single one of the children. I've met him several times and heard glowing testimonials from other colleagues. They *knew* he was joking, and he would never have risked it otherwise. He'd taught them for years and there was an intense and affectionate relationship that had grown over those years. They knew he cared, they knew he could teach, and they all knew the boundaries. It is one of the treasures of teaching, especially with older children, that you can develop this bond, but it is a bond built on enormously strong mutual expectations and relationship cues. This is not day 1 language with students you do not know.

This is what is possible – albeit at the edge of possibility. Never mistake the *outcome* of sustained relationship building with the *methods* required to achieve it. Or to put it another way, when someone loves you and you love them back, then you can say *I love you*. But saying *I love you* to someone does not make them feel the same way. The outcome is not the method.

---

60 You are not Coco the Fun Teacher. You do not have a van painted with Disney characters that you drive to children's parties, where you make balloon animals and pretend your thumb has vanished. Coco the Fun Teacher is the polar opposite of the Mary Poppins teacher. For more on this, see my forthcoming book *Running the Circus*.

GOOD RELATIONSHIPS ARE BUILT OUT OF STRUCTURES AND HIGH EXPECTATIONS.

The teacher-student relationship is important, but it is built on trust – and trust is built on mutually predictable behaviour. And that requires sincerely executed norms and routines.

But we do not expect students to only behave when they have a strong relationship with all staff. The expectation is that students should behave well because it is the right thing to do.

CHAPTER 10
SILENCE

Promote quiet classrooms these days and people see you as a dinosaur encouraging a return to the 1950s. But quiet fosters calm work and focus and frees students to think and create. Skilful teachers craft moments of quiet for students to listen and to generate learning intensity. Old fashioned? Absolutely not.

Kevin Knight, director of the New Zealand Graduate School of Education[61]

How quiet do you want them? One thing I have learned is that students will take their behavioural cues about what is acceptable from many sources, but principally the teacher and one another. If the teacher never challenges them about a behaviour, they tend to think it is acceptable. If a teacher never challenges them when the class is in riotous voice, then they learn to accept this as normal. If the teacher constantly tackles them when they break a silence, they learn that this is normal too. I've seen schools in the most difficult circumstances with silent corridors. And I've seen schools brimming with affluent, well-educated children shouting merrily without purpose through lessons. You *can* get students to be as quiet as you need them to be.

There is an old episode of *Star Trek* where Captain Kirk, the libertine commander of the Starship *Enterprise,* finds himself stranded on a planet with nothing but natural resources to help him avoid being flattened by an enormous alien intent on his demise. In one memorable scene, he helplessly scoops up handfuls of precious stones that litter the ground there as abundantly as granite or sandstone chippings on Earth. Helpfully for the viewing audience, he narrates his predicament into his tricorder:

> A large deposit of diamonds on the surface. Perhaps the hardest substance known in the universe. Beautifully crystallised and pointed, but too small to be useful as a weapon. An incredible fortune in stones yet I would trade them all for a hand phaser, or a good solid club.[62]

---

61 Correspondence with the author.
62 *Arena,* Star Trek: The Original Series, Stardate: 3045.6, Original Airdate: 19 Jan, 1967

What would be a king's ransom of wealth on Earth was useless in his situation. Value is not intrinsic to any object; its value is always contextual. It depends on what you need and where you are. When you need it, it becomes more valuable. This is the law of supply and demand, even in unnamed planets on the final frontier of the Alpha Quadrant. Silence by itself is not *intrinsically* valuable. It is only ever *contextually* valuable. Understanding what these contexts are is essential. It's valuable if you need it, and if the students need it. Which is the same as saying 'when you need it'.

When is it valuable?

One of the most important skills you can teach a student is *when* to be quiet, and to teach them the habit of being so. There are many things they need to be able to do in order to succeed: read, listen, think hard. These things can be done with noise, but they are usually better done without.

One reason for this is that people are not, as is commonly believed, multitaskers. We hear this often – children frequently refer to it. Ambitious adults festoon their CVs with claims of high aptitude in this area. Sadly, what we know about the science of learning, and the brain, suggest that this is not what we do at all.

The myth of multitasking

We don't multitask so much as task-switch. Our brains have a very limited bandwidth of focus available to them. We can only think about a few things at once, and the fewer we focus on, the better the quality of that focus. You might see a teenager, apparently hard at work. But they're surfing Wikipedia, while chatting on Facebook, making a podcast, listening to music on their headphones, watching television, and doing their homework. When you challenge them on it, they say, 'I'm multitasking! God!'

Feel free to tell them that they are doing no such thing; they are task-*switching*, which is to say, thinking about one thing after another in a sequential but fragmented and inefficient way.

Research[63] suggests there is an enormous cognitive cost to be paid for thinking like this: focus atrophies; retention dwindles; time is lost between every task

---

63 Kirschner, P. and Bruyckere, P. de (2017) 'The myths of the digital native and the multitasker', *Teaching and Teacher Education: An International Journal of Research and Studies* 67 (1), 135-142. Elsevier Ltd. Retrieved June 25, 2020 from www.bit.ly/3qljiS2

due to changing from one thought process to another. It's like trying to write a song while pogo-sticking on a trampoline in a lift. Focus is a very finite real estate. This is also why I have to turn the car radio off in order to reverse. Too much distraction.[64]

So, far from being the plea of vicious pedagogues everywhere, silence really is golden for students. The key is knowing when and where to deploy it. In a library, it's very useful, because people need to read and think. In a playground, it's not so useful, although you will still need to set maximum levels of noise and obtain quiet at times, e.g. when lining up. Of course, mileage varies and this is not an exact science.

In a corridor? Opinion is divided. The difference seems to be context. If your corridors are civil, students walk briskly between lessons, noise is low, and people are safe, then it may not be as important to enforce absolute silence. However if none of these conditions are met, it *might* be a useful strategy to consider quiet corridors. Some might say, 'Why not just very quiet? Talking is natural,' and they may have a point. But it is much harder to teach normally rowdy children to be merely quiet rather than silent, because any level of conversation encourages a reversion to the old habits. It is far, far easier to start with silence, because it is easily understood and perceived, and its absence is much easier to discern and monitor. But once achieved reliably, you can think about allowing sensible levels of conversation.

There are some who consider expecting complete quiet to be an act of oppression, but asking children to be absolutely silent for short periods of time is perfectly acceptable. People are expected to be silent in many circumstances that no one gets upset about: cinemas, theatres, music performances, libraries, in court, beat-poetry nights and Remembrance Sunday. It is not to everyone's taste, but it is a perfectly normal and healthy behaviour to practise. To turn it around, I would be more concerned if the children we taught were *not* capable of being silent for a few minutes at a time.[65]

---

64 This is such a powerful conviction; I sincerely believe I will reverse off a ramp into the void if I don't turn off drive-time banter. I refuse to test this hypothesis.

65 A small number of people are so concerned about this that they consider such an expectation abusive, which only makes me wonder what adjectives they reserve for actual abusiveness. Hyperbole corrodes this debate and we should make it our professional ambition to avoid such absurdities.

A quiet place

Silence is a very, very useful quality for lessons. Teachers need to settle excitable hearts. Calm spaces must be created. Focus must be gathered. The subject must be taken seriously, Instructions must be given. Answers made and shared. Students must listen to one another and learn to treat each other as valuable members of their learning community. Thinking and reading must be done. Students need to know when to switch silence on and off like a tap. That's the trick, and the goal. The aim is not to teach them to be monks. This is not a seminary.[66] The aim is to teach them to be behaviourally versatile, and to recognise the need for such behaviours, and when to use them, like sailors manage their sails: when to tack and when to gybe, when to dodge the boom and when to splice the mainbrace.[67]

So every teacher should make the teaching of the habit of silence uppermost in their behaviour curriculum. It is a gateway skill, in the same way that literacy is a gateway skill to further learning. Being able to be silent, to reflect, mediate, think and focus with purpose is as important as being able to talk with focus and purpose.

Teach students how to be silent, and teach them how to talk

We return to one of our earliest principles: good behaviour must be taught, not told.

The things we want them to do are not natural to them. If we don't teach them to do the things we want, don't be surprised if some of them perform them better than others. And don't be surprised if the difference between these two groups rests on their differing personal circumstances, backgrounds and inheritance.

What kind of speaking skills do we need to teach?

If you want students to be good at a particular activity, it is best to teach them that activity. Generic skills are slowly falling out of fashion as a teaching aim these days, because mounting evidence suggests that many things that we think transfer into different domains actually do not.[68] It used to be claimed,

---

66 Unless you *do* teach in a seminary, in which case please read my book *Running the Chancel*.

67 You can read more about this in my new book, *Running the Man o' War*.

68 Tricot, A. and Sweller, J. (2013) 'Domain-Specific Knowledge and Why Teaching Generic Skills Does Not Work', *Educational Psychology Review* 26. 10.1007/s10648-013-9243-1.

for example, that Latin was a useful thing to learn because (it was believed) the logicality and structure of the language would transfer into different areas of the students' thinking, and they would become more logical thinkers. But this is not the case, and there is no demonstrable gain to be made to learning Latin, other than increased aptitude at Latin, and an appreciation of how it influences modern languages. Which isn't a criticism, but simply a recalibration of why it might be valuable.

The same is true for those parents who play Mozart to children in the womb, in the belief that getting them to appreciate classical music will help encourage brain development.[69] Or the belief that learning to play an instrument makes one better at maths. Again, there is no evidence to suggest this.

Similarly, if you want children to be good at, for example, group work, then teach them the specific protocols and etiquette that makes group work successful. Namely, teach them about different roles in groups, teach them what they should actually do throughout the process, and what their part will be at the beginning, middle and end. This is crucial, because unless they receive training, many adults also struggle with high-quality group work.[70]

So if you want children to learn how to debate, then explicitly teach them the ground rules, and convey your expectations to them in this by constant behavioural cues, by consequences, and by challenge. Teach each activity as if it were separate from every other one.

- How to make a point of information

- How to argue a point logically

- How to counter-argue

- How to wait your turn

- How to listen and take notes on the opposing side

---

69   The so-called *Mozart effect*, fisked and buried in this joyously-named piece: Pietschnig, J., Voracek, M. and Formann, A. (2010) 'Mozart effect–Shmozart effect: A meta-analysis', *Intelligence* 38, pp. 314–323. 10.1016/j.intell.2010.03.001.

70   In my experience, they often end up producing less than they would have done separately. And one person gets the coffee.

Show them examples of each behaviour. Get them to demonstrate what each might look like. Correct them and suggest improvements. Repeat the process. Get them to self-evaluate. Teach them how to debate by teaching them the component behaviours of debating.

If you want children to be good at contributing answers in class, set your expectations out early, and tell them exactly how it is to be achieved (Hands up? No hands up? Waving a towel?), what you expect (no huffing and puffing, or straining, or any other sound beloved of the keen or attention-seeking), no disappointment expressed, no eyes rolling or bitter sighs. Tell them what will happen if they do not contribute. Perhaps you operate a cold calling system[71] (where students are asked to contribute without warning)[72] so that students will be expected to listen.

The point is that these behaviours are not obvious. None of them are. They are classroom and school specific. They are the types of behaviours they may not even use in the rest of their lives (how many children put their hands up to ask a question at home?), so the teacher should assume that instructional effort will need to be invested in order to see success in these areas. **Once again: we want to make it easy to behave, and hard to misbehave.**

To conclude: students must be as quiet as you think they need to be. If that is most of the lesson, then fine. If you have long extended periods where they can talk, that's fine too. But what is non-negotiable is that the conversation must substantially lean into the learning, and any conversations that take the students away from that too much must be discouraged or used with care.

Talking with purpose and with focus is an invaluable habit. It is too easy to succumb to doing only what we consider pleasant. It is important to teach children how to commit to any task, even if its novelty and amusement are not immediately apparent. Many of our greatest achievements are achieved not through constantly delightful activities, but through tasks requiring effort and persistence, from passing an exam to running a marathon. Few successes are given to us by accident, unless you win the lottery. Most of what we value

---

71 Lemov, D. (2010) *Teach like a champion: 49 techniques that put students on the path to college*. San Francisco: Jossey-Bass.

72 Or perhaps you use lollipop sticks to decide who answers next, presumably because you lack the ability to make any decision, however small. I can only imagine how hard it must be for you at a buffet.

is achieved by a combination of talent, good fortune, and hard work. And hard work is the one we have the most control over.

Remember Paul, speaking in Romans:'For what I want to do I do not do, but what I hate I do. And if I do what I do not want to do, I agree that the law is good.'

It is important to teach children not to simply succumb to their immediate desires, but to learn to deny oneself gratification in order to achieve a greater goal. Then they truly grasp a sense of themselves as moral beings that exist over time, rather than as helpless creatures of the moment, dumb vessels of hedonism.

Remember, flourishing is not happiness. Flourishing *can* often incidentally bring happiness. But satisfaction is a greater goal worth pursuing, not only of ourselves, but for the sake of others also. Knowing how to be silent isn't the mark of a conquered or broken spirit; it is the sign of self-mastery, and the gateway of so much that we value. When we know how to be quiet, we can start to learn how to be loud. And that makes us powerful.

STUDENTS ARE SOCIAL BEINGS

No man (or woman) is an island. Our behaviour is strongly influenced by other people. Other people and their opinions matter to us. If you teach a class, you teach a group, and group dynamics are not the same as solo or pair behaviour.

CHAPTER 11
MANNERS

Manners maketh man.

William Horman

People being what they are, offence will often be given and taken in classrooms.[73] Sometimes it will be deliberate on the part of the student, which is to say rudeness. What do you do then?

As ever, the first thing to remember is to create a culture where rudeness is less likely. Make it easier for students to be polite. How?

Manners musteth be taught

First of all, by clearly defining, long in advance, what good manners mean in the classroom. 'Manners maketh man,'[74] as the saying goes. But manners are not universal. In Japan, eating on the street is frowned upon; but looking at central London on a Saturday night, you'd think there was nowhere else it was allowed. Some people think that to be polite, one must track a speaker with their eyes. And some cultures view eye contact as rude. Appropriate etiquette is very contextual, because rituals aren't always logical, but born out of aesthetics, tradition and taste.

As the teacher, you must *define* manners if you want to maketh little men and women. Remember that some students will view coming into the lesson within ten minutes of the starter bell as perfectly punctual. Some students think that mockery is fine as long as it's 'banter'. Some students see no problem with asking the teacher if they're married, or gay, straight or on drugs.[75]

---

73 In fact you can just take the words 'in classrooms' right out and the sentence is more accurate.

74 And woman. From *Vulgaria* by Horman, W. (1975) *Theatrum Orbis Terrarum*, W. J. Johnson edition. Horman, a 15th/16th-century head of Eton and Winchester, was considered somewhat of a controversialist, having been a principal antagonist of the Grammarians' Wars, which if you *have* to fight in a war, is probably one of the best ones to be in. 'Manners maketh man' is of course also the maxim of Harry Hart, a loyal Kingsman.

75 Or all four at once.

Students will benefit from clarification about such matters very early on. Demonstrate the type of conduct you want to see; draw attention to it; discuss it; congratulate students when it occurs, and challenge them when it does not; but first of all and most of all, help them understand what manners mean to you. You might be the first person they have met who makes an issue of it.

What are manners?

Why do manners maketh anything? Aren't they pointless? One of the best definitions I have heard is that having good manners means 'treating the other person as if they matter'. That is both profound and simple. When I was a secondary teacher, I spent a term at the University of Cambridge as a teaching fellow, a programme designed to promote state school application to Oxbridge colleges. Part of the role involved attending the occasional formal function, which induced in me skyscraping levels of social anxiety and imposter syndrome.

But one thing struck me: how consummately mannered many of the people I met at these events were. One of the college masters had spent his career in the diplomatic corps, and I watched, fascinated, as he glided around the room being glisteningly charming to a hundred people, instantly, whoever they were. Everyone received a purposeful handshake, eye contact, and a sincere, personalised enquiry. It was mesmerising to watch. Something that would paralyse many, done so easily. Manners in this example made me feel welcomed and included.

Manners can define membership – or its opposite – of a social group; as a tribal signifier, they can divide as well as unite. In my time at Cambridge I remember sitting at the High Table for dinner and being seated opposite from a well-known alumnus and writer. His first question – his *first* question – was, 'And what school did you go to?' The second I mentioned Boclair Academy, a lovely but distinctly *not* famous comprehensive school, rather than a grand and ancient private institution, he completely lost interest. In this case, manners were a way to filter out anyone alien to his tribe.[76]

But at their core, manners are about knowing social norms and observing them in order to maintain cordial relations with others. As with silence, the reason

---

76   For clarity, I should mention that my experience was almost 100% positive, and everyone from porter to master were avatars of kindness and politeness. Snobbery was a weed in the garden, not the garden itself.

why it is important that students are aware of these and can use them is that, in the world, it is important to have the flexibility to move in and out of different social contexts with ease, and to navigate through society and societies. It is to be sensitive to the tastes and sensitivities of others in order to decide when to offend or not, rather than blundering through every encounter like the Hulk.

The joy I used to feel whenever one of our students from inner-city London made it to a university was equalled only by my dismay whenever one dropped out because they felt like they couldn't cope being somewhere other than the neighbourhood they grew up in. Never underestimate the invisible advantages that upbringing can convey.

The *Up* series is a sequence of extraordinary documentary films produced by Granada Television for ITV that has followed the lives of 14 British children since 1964, when they were seven years old. To date, the documentary has had nine episodes – one every seven years – across 56 years. There were broadly two groups of children, one composed mostly of middle-class children, and one composed of working-class children.

Watching the early episodes, it is impossible not to notice the enormous differences in expectation and aspiration that exist even in the seven-year-olds. Some of them had their lives already charted, from prep school right through to the law firm they would aspire to be partners in. Some of the kids from more modest backgrounds thought they'd probably end up as cowboys or taxi drivers. Even at that tender age, many children have clear ideas about who they can and cannot be. Our job is often to correct that. Life will present enough obstacles in the paths of many children; it is important that we remove at least the bars created in the cages of their minds.

Manners also maketh you

Another strategy that makes it easier for children *not* to be rude is to manage your own language and emotional state carefully. If you use sarcasm and the student doesn't get it, or isn't on the right wavelength to receive it, they may think you're taking the mickey, and respond in kind, possibly escalating as they do so. If you shout at a student, don't be surprised if they shout back. Why shouldn't they? You've demonstrated that this is acceptable behaviour. Back a kid into a corner and see what they do. Also, if a student is used to angry battles at home, then don't be surprised if they interpret aggression aggressively, and put their armour on.

In other words, one of the best ways to encourage good manners, and discourage rudeness, is to be polite yourself. Measured, calm, positive and focused. In many ways, students need you to be the best version of you, the professional you.

But even assuming that you're in charge of yourself – you're positive, clear and mannered – the children are still rude at times. What then?

1. First, don't jump to conclusions. Judge if you think their response was meant to be rude, or if they've expressed themselves clumsily. Children are often unsophisticated in their language choices. If you ask a five-year-old what they're having for dinner, and they shout 'Poo!' or something, it's certainly inappropriate, but it might not be aimed at you. Or if you ask them to speak, and they sigh with a 'Fucking hell' or similar under their breath, it might not be intended as an attack on you. Of course, both of these need an appropriate – maybe a strong – response, but it may not always be as serious as a student looking you in the eye and telling you to fuck off.

   In a case like this, you might want to explain to them that their choice of wording wasn't right, and you'd like them to reconsider what they should have said. This might be done in front of the class, so they understand that the behaviour has been challenged, or it might need a more serious chat after lessons. Or it might need a sanction, or an escalation. The point is, try to factor in intentions *as well as* outcomes, not instead of. This avoids escalating unnecessarily for something that can be dealt with conversationally.

   At the beginning of a relationship with a student or class, you might need a few conversations like this. Many students will appreciate you explaining to them what you prefer. Getting to know one another is part of the process. But make it clear that you expect them not to say/do 'that' again, or you'll treat it as intentional, and deal with it accordingly.

   I used to have a lot of conversations with my students about this. I found that five minutes of explaining to them that yes, fucking hell *is* an inappropriate phrase in a classroom, and then making it clear that they needed to choose better words, was worth a lot of pain later on.

2. If you are reasonably sure it was intentional and directed at someone, then it is far more serious. The dignity of all members of the class is

fundamental – these rights we hold to be self-evident. Which means treating everyone as if they mattered, because they *do*. Which means that insults and rudeness have no place in the classroom.

If a student is clearly deliberately rude, then they need a reprimand. That might range from a public rebuke to being asked to leave the room for a short period if the offence is extreme. It must be taken seriously, and the class need to see that it is serious. If a student is allowed to behave in this way, and the teacher tries to sweep it under the carpet, perhaps accepting a haughty and insincere sorry from the student, then they normalise it. They show students that you can indeed tell the teacher to go fuck themselves, so long as you mumble an apology five minutes later that you obviously don't have to mean.

If you have to remove them, send the student to a prearranged place as per your systems with the minimum of fuss. The rest of the class need to see that rudeness – to you especially – is a very serious matter, and the best way to discourage it is to treat it seriously every time it happens.

Then at some point in the day – preferably as soon as possible – the student needs to receive a school sanction, plus some form of pastoral conversation with you. As usual, this must include:

▷ An apology.

▷ An explanation, if necessary.

▷ A discussion about what needs to happen next/what behaviour would be better.

▷ A clear indication about what will happen if the behaviour is repeated.

▷ A clear communication that you want the student to do better and want to see their behaviour improve.

This is a minimum, and anything less than even this loose structure risks repetition of the behaviour, or worse, a reinforcement of the behaviour as acceptable.

That's the response to rudeness. But don't forget to promote positive manners, i.e. teach them what constitutes good manners. I worked with a school in Spain where children came from family backgrounds so difficult that many of them had never had a meal with their family at a table. So the school set up a small dining room that was dressed like a family home, and every day a small group of children had to sit at the table and have breakfast or brunch with the senior staff, learning about cutlery, eating etiquette, and crucially, the million ways that people connect and converse over food.

Because manners mean so many things, it's impossible to list everything that children should learn. I leave that to you. But remember these basic points:

- Students need to see concrete examples of what constitutes good manners.

- They need it to be taught.

- And they need you to tell them specific things to do, and not to do.

For example, make holding doors open an expectation on all students; or a hearty good morning; or a handshake; or *please* and *thank-you*; or *please may I*; or offering to help before someone asks you to; or bringing three pens (*one to use, one to lose, one to lend*).

Or a million other acts of courtesy that make life so much better. It has to start somewhere, and if it hasn't started for some of your children, then you need to be the one who lights that fire for them. You're the fire starter.

CHAPTER 12
THE ROOM WHERE IT HAPPENS: TRUANCY AND LATENESS

Truancy

If a student isn't in your lesson, they aren't learning. If they miss learning, they find it harder to keep up with the syllabus, which puts greater pressure on them, and increases the likelihood they will misbehave, or choose not to attend in the future. Bunking lessons can become a habit too, and harder to break once it is embedded.

Some teachers treat a badly behaved student's absence as a bit of a relief, a holiday from their capers. But it is not a holiday: it is building up problems for the future. A diligent pupil being off for a day or two won't cause too much trouble if they get notes and some catch-up time. A difficult or less able student will be thrown even further behind, academically and socially, by the same loss.

So treat any absence as a mystery to be solved. Find out why they missed the lesson. Some schools' communication systems can be a little slow, or disorganised. Sometimes people forget to pass on messages, or clearly communicate why a pupil is off. Make it your business to know.

If a student misses a lesson, mark it on your daily register. You should *always* keep a register. If you don't, you don't really know who's been, and when, and missed what. You might think you do, but you have too many things to think about. You *will* forget (see 'Records', p. 153).

Multiple absences will merge into one and you'll think students have been in more than they have. A register is a tool to work out who comes to your lessons. Look at it after a few weeks and see if there are any patterns. You will notice that one student has missed an entire unit. Or perhaps they've missed the beginning to three units, which means their subsequent learning is probably not so secure. You may find that a student is always absent every Friday. Why? Is something going on at home?

Legitimate absence is fine, as long as you know what happened, and what is being done to at least try to remedy the learning loss. The student needs to feel that they matter. This is not just a learning consideration, but a social and behavioural one too. Imagine missing a day at work, and when you come back, no one mentions it. You would surmise that people didn't care if you were there or not. Now imagine that circumstance as a child who has a crummy home life and doesn't think school cares about him. Then they realise that they're right, and people either don't mind or actively prefer their absence. That can have a huge impact on their attitude to learning, and whether or not they bother to turn up in future.[77]

Schools are full of small places that no one sees. Even the best designed schools have nooks and crannies – let alone the legendary bike sheds – for students to vanish into. Plenty of students have worked out that they can miss almost all of their learning time and no one will say anything. Some students have even worked out that they can bunk an entire day's worth of lessons in a large school if they simply tell every teacher that stops them, that another teacher has sent them on an errand. I've had kids tell me this was their tactic for years – not days, *years*.[78] (The remedy to this, incidentally, is to insist upon a whole-school policy of requiring notes or passes for any absence from lessons, to be presented upon request. With *no* exceptions. If this bucket has even one hole, it's useless.)

But someone has to care enough to check; and if you come across a student out of lessons, it is an act of compassion to check their story. And if it's not true, you must follow up. That means either arranging an extracurricular conversation, calling home, informing a pastoral manager, a form tutor etc. Not only is there the issue of bunking to unpick and hopefully fix, but the student learns to lie as a survival habit.

You'll be back

If the students know that *you* will be absent, and another, less familiar teacher is covering your lesson, then this is when many students will plan a truancy like jailbirds plotting an escape. So prep for your absence: make sure you give them meaningful work and leave a seating plan. Ask the teacher to take a register, and

---

77 This is another reason why it is good to talk to every student in every lesson, no matter what. Say hello to them by name. Mention their work. Ask them a question. Say their name and make eye contact. Let them feel like you noticed them. For the lonely, the daunted or the student on the edge, it can be like water in a desert.

78 I like to imagine there are whole cohorts of children who live under the floorboards, between the pipes and in the false ceiling, like Borrowers.

then follow up with any gaps. Leave as few blind spots as possible. Students will find them quickly. Human nature is incredibly clever, tenacious and wily. Like water, children find a way through the gaps. So leave as few as possible. One tip I mentioned in *Running the Room* is useful here: assign roles to your students in the event of a cover. Teach one student to hand out books or collect work in; task another with giving the supply teacher the seating plan or even the work; and ask another to take a shadow register of those present and absent. A little sowing will reap a fine harvest. (See 'Cover lessons', p. 119)

And never forget to find out why unplanned absences happen. Why are they off? Usually it's simple work avoidance or meeting up for social reasons with their peers. Fine. I mean, *not* fine, but not too serious, and this can be dealt with by normal means – conversations about attendance, calls home, sanctions, behaviour plans, closer monitoring etc.

But there may also be a serious reason: fear of a classmate; mental health issues; addiction; bullying; pyromania; abuse etc. Most of us live most of our lives in private; like icebergs, we are largely submerged, and what others see is the tip. Scratch with your fingernail at many people's lives and you will uncover depths both happy and tragic. The symptoms of our hinterlands are often mundane but hide more serious circumstances. So take truancy seriously. The student has not vanished. They continue to exist outside of our perceptions, like a thought experiment.

These problems are better addressed if you diligently take a serious interest in your absent students. And always communicate what you find out to your line management. Let the school know, so that people with more direct responsibility for their pastoral care can use that information to discern greater or more serious patterns, and act upon that intelligence.

Summary:

- *Keep a close track of who, then find out why.*

- *Truancy burns learning, and leads to misbehaviour as they fall behind.*

- *Set serious work for planned absences.*

- *Truancy often hides greater problems.*

Lateness
What'd I miss?

It will not surprise anyone to hear that the less time a child spends in a classroom, the less impact teaching has. Being in the room where it happens matters. Of course, what happens in the room matters too, but for now let's focus on being there in the first place. Lateness, like its troublesome cousin truancy, is a blight.

- First, it obviously reduces the time spent learning.

- Second, it means that students miss vital instructions that will help them to access the rest of the lesson, ruining the quality of the time that they do spend there.

Lateness is misbehaviour. It is not trivial, or just a nuisance. It damages the child's education, and that of others, and wrecks the flow of the lesson. Obviously there may be some genuine reasons to be late, but the norm of being on time must be emphasised as much as possible.

How to reduce lateness
Proactively:

- Teach students the importance of being on time, explicitly. It may seem obvious, but to many children, it's not apparent why a few minutes matter, or what harm it does. Create a communal understanding that it harms people.

- Teach children what punctuality means. Define it exactly. What does late mean to you? What does being on time to the airport mean? To dinner? To a friend's house? 'Late' is a subjective term. It needs hammering down, or children will exploit this vagueness, deliberately or innocently.

- Teach them how to be on time. This may mean discussing what to do to finish the previous lesson promptly, or what kind of behaviours between lessons make people late. When should they go to the toilet? When should they get their bags or visit their lockers? What routes are best? What should they be doing or thinking about three minutes before the end of break? And so on.

- Teach them the corridor/queuing procedures. Teach them the entry procedures.

The more these are discussed and taught as habits, the more likely it is that children will see punctuality as important, achievable, and personally relevant.

Reactively: This is important to think about. How will you deal with a late student? There are various possible responses, bearing in mind that this is taking place once the lesson has started and you will be occupied doing other things. You could:

- Direct students to take their seats silently and begin as best as possible. This has the benefit of maintaining lesson flow, but risks normalising lateness, as students might think there is no consequence to their actions. Counteract this by making sure there is a guaranteed conversation at the end of the lesson/break/day about their lateness. There may be a sanction attached to this, to deter future lateness. Make sure the class is aware of this process, so they expect it, and understand that lateness is unacceptable.

- Expect students to produce a note justifying their lateness. For example, another teacher may have detained them for a legitimate reason. Without a note, an automatic penalty should occur.

- Have a stand-up row with them for their lateness. This is entertaining for the class, but probably not a good option, as you direct the whole class attention to one student's misbehaviour. It creates an audience for the student, which can have a negative effect on the quality of their response. They may feel threatened, or hostile, or embarrassed, or even emboldened by being centre stage.

- Say something witty and sarcastic. But much as I enjoy the benefits of a healthy (and sometimes) humorous relationship with classes, that relationship is not achieved simply by being (in your eyes) witty. This gets the process back to front. You can have light-hearted banter with students *when* they trust you to be responsible and trustworthy – and when you trust them with that communication. Not before.

Humour is a delicate thing. *Your* sense of humour is not necessarily *their* sense of humour. What you find trivial and amusing, they may find baffling, or deadly serious. If they misinterpret your humour, they may feel you are making fun of them, or abusing your institutional authority. This then makes it more likely they will respond with anger, sarcasm or mockery. Which in turn presents the teacher with a higher-level behaviour to contend with, which the class will rightly be watching closely.

So, make it as easy to behave as you can. I suggest you:

- Minimise disruption by avoiding a melodramatic confrontation.

- Allow the student to enter discreetly in some way.

- Acknowledge the lateness minimally but make sure that it is publicly noted.

- Always follow up.

- Accept nothing but the most serious of excuses – if you simply let it slide for trivial reasons, students will see punctuality as trivial.

- Always ask for evidence of this excuse – remember that even if you trust the student, asking for some kind of substantiation creates the expectation that students won't simply be allowed to say, 'Mr Jenkins kept me behind.' If you do not, the wiliest of students will quickly learn this is how you slither out of a penalty.

- Make students catch up missed time, and as a default set sanctions to indicate to the class that lateness is unacceptable.

Of course, lateness may also be indicative of some other issue. They may be avoiding lessons, or detained by bullies, or sick, or coping with some personal difficulty. In the discussion afterwards, it is important that space is made for an investigation, however light touch, so that any such matters can be uncovered and dealt with. But for the most part, lateness is usually caused by the most obvious reasons: laziness, chatting with friends, luxurious toilet breaks, lesson avoidance and so on. So make punctuality the norm, and make exceptions only when 100% necessary.

CHAPTER 13

COVER LESSONS

Cover lessons are notoriously difficult. A teacher, often unfamiliar with the class (and sometimes the subject, the topic or the school), is asked to direct and teach a room full of bubbling, egotistical agents of chaos. Children frequently take the path of least resistance, and least effort. And why not? It's an entirely rational thing to do, maybe even the most sensible. Why expend effort on things that don't satisfy perceived goals? Even the diligent student will see the possibilities for loafing and work avoidance in a cover lesson. I once walked into a supply teacher's lesson to find one of my best year 11 students simply reading a *Harry Potter* book. 'Why aren't you doing the classwork?' I asked. She just pointed at the instructions on the board, that read, 'Write a poem about who you want to be when you grow up.' She stared at me like a hostage, and I imagined her blinking 'Save me' in Morse code.[79]

Expertise in one area rarely transfers easily into another. A great science teacher may not be a great geography teacher, or PE teacher. 'Teaching' has some common skills, but many that are not common to all subjects. Expectations of behaviour vary too. A drama teacher may perceive some movement and conversation as normal, but a history teacher may not. Children sense this uncertainty. They know when they are in a grey area. It is entirely rational for them to exploit this. I don't mean *moral*, just *rational* and therefore understandable. And predictable.

Setting a cover lesson

I am frequently asked what teachers should do in order to guarantee a good lesson or class when they are away. Many teachers complain that if they take a day off, the class devolves into a brute state. But you cannot control anyone remotely. You *can* create conditions where good behaviour is more likely, either by moulding the students' values, habits, expectations etc., or by leaving them with prompts that encourage the right behaviour. And to a very large extent, good behaviour in cover lessons is a whole-school, leadership issue. There is only so much you can do personally.

---

79 For clarity: the students must still expect to do the work set, and you need to create that expectation explicitly. But you'd have to have a heart of stone not to sympathise.

So how can we get the best behaviour and the most effort and focus from the class when we aren't there?

Firstly, a lot of the work is done long before you need to set a cover lesson.

- Teach the class how to behave in a normal lesson: norms, routines, consequences, values, habits etc. This helps to ensure that they are as aware as possible what the norms are, and how to behave. If there is normally ambiguity and inconsistency, that will be magnified in the more fluid circumstances of a cover lesson.

- Teach the class specifically what the behavioural expectations are *for cover lessons*, long in advance of when you need to. Make it clear that cover lessons are also your lessons; work you leave is part of your curriculum. That they need to try hard, just like normal. That they should be civil, cooperative and so on, just like normal.

- Assign specific roles to named students: one to hand out books and paper; another to distribute equipment; one to collect it in; one to help the cover teacher; one to summon help if needed; one to give them the seating plan; and so on.

- Let your class know what kinds of behaviours are specifically prohibited, for example:

  ▷ Asking to leave the room repeatedly

  ▷ Sitting in the wrong seat

  ▷ Pretending not to understand

  ▷ Shouting out

  ▷ Low effort

And so on. What often happens is that the teacher is absent one day, the children find out a few minutes before the lesson, half of them get excited and shout, 'Yes! It's a free lesson!' and anarchy reigns. Even the ones who would normally try hard think, 'Oh bugger, here we go again,' and reach for their *Hunger Games* worry beads.

Treat your work seriously

If you set work, expect to see it when you get back, and follow up on what hasn't been done. If you don't demonstrate to the class that it is noticed, marked and assessed, they will learn that it is not important. They will think it is holding pattern work. It is busywork. It is pointless. And they will be right. The very diligent will do it, but with less effort, and everyone else will do it a little or not at all.

One good way to ensure that the class sees the work as meaningful is to set high-status, meaningful work. Unless it is an emergency, work should be set with as much care as any other lesson. I've seen some dreadful pieces of cover work that barely qualify as an activity: 'Draw your hand' for art, or its English equivalent, 'Write a poem about something.' Colouring-in tasks in RE; watching *Mulan* to 'learn about China'. Work like that screams *I am pointless* to the kids. Don't set it, or you contribute to children's perception that cover lessons aren't high-quality lessons.

Try to communicate with the person taking your class, if you can. Ask them to supply a list of names of students who need to receive a consequence, or redo work, or a call home or whatever you see fit. Children need to feel that the work and the cover lesson is high status. If it is perceived as low status, there is a far lower chance of children focusing on it.

Remember, *make it easy for them to behave.*

Taking a cover lesson

This is the harder situation. You might be at the mercy of the work you have been set. You may not know the class or the topic. Or you may know some of these things, or partially know them. If you are covering lessons in your own school, you may already know them a little, and you may know the covered teacher.

- First of all, preparation is useful. If you can, familiarise yourself with the room, the lesson set, the seats, the seating plan. Get as much information as you can.

- Be at the classroom door before they arrive *if* you can.

- Get them to line up if that's the school policy, or if you want them to. Use that time to settle them, get their uniform sorted, or give any other instruction you need to convey that this is *your room, your rules,* and this is a *real lesson.*

- Get them to go into the lesson slowly and orderly. Either ask them to sit where you assign them, or to follow the existing seating plan if you have one. This all suggests subtle dominance; it conveys that this is not, despite their hopes, a free lesson, or play time. Getting them to put their planners/diaries/folders on their desks will help with names.[80]

- Settle the class. Create a transition moment, where you explicitly explain the basic premises of the room, and your relationship with them. Children very quickly get a sense of whether or not the cover teacher is taking it seriously, or if they are simply enduring until the bell. So give them the right impression.

- Give them your instructions for how everyone will proceed. This is usually a shortened version of the introductory speech I recommended in *Running the Room*. The beats are all the same, compressed:

  ▷ Welcome to the lesson.

  ▷ Lessons are important things.

  ▷ You will be learning today. I look forward to seeing what you know and what you can do.

  ▷ I expect you to behave.

  ▷ Here's what that means.

  ▷ I'll help you if I can.

  ▷ If you don't try your best, there will be consequences, involving your classroom teacher and me.

  ▷ I want you to succeed.

Simple points to make, but often forgotten. A lot of children, once they hear this, will at least understand that these are the standard terms and conditions of the

---

80   There is usually one comedian who pretends to be someone else. Normally they pretend to be a nice, quiet kid who won't object or speak up when they have to swap seats.

classroom, and acquiesce to a lesser or greater degree. Many children experience nothing but the weakest forms of cover lesson, where the teacher vainly points to the work on the board and bellows at them occasionally when the mayhem becomes impossible to ignore. Many are happy to simply last until the end, and the kids know it. Like water, it's easier to take the path of least resistance. The children know it too. So we need to make it as hard as possible to fail.

Make it as hard as possible to fail

If children openly and aggressively test the boundaries early in the cover lesson, give them a warning and try to divert their attention to the work, but remember that you are facing a much shorter timeframe than the regular teacher, who is building a long game with the class. If a student has aggressively or repeatedly misbehaved, have them removed quickly, parked somewhere else, and follow up later.

If you allow one or two students to set the tone early on, the rest of the lesson will feel like chaos, because it is unlikely they will reform themselves. But if the loudest of mouths are removed quickly, the rest of the class will see that you mean business. So summon help quickly, and don't feel bad about it. Lots of teachers feel bad asking for help. I understand this, having been a teacher who never asked for help. Why? Because I didn't want to look weak – like the one who couldn't cope. Ironically, by not asking for help I was a) demonstrating that I *wasn't* coping and b) making it more likely that things would get worse and I would cope even less.

It's strangely obvious to any experienced teacher that being unafraid to ask for help is part of a healthy, functioning school system, not a dysfunctional one. But when you are new, or anxious about your image, these things don't seem obvious. In fact, many of the things I recommend as good practice might seem obvious once you've been doing them for a while but are clearly not obvious enough for everyone to actually do them, routinely and consistently.

Throughout the lesson, help students as best you can, considering this may not be your subject strength. Be honest when you come up against your limits. Ask for help from more able students and share what you find. Most children will see that as a sign of good sense and strength, not weakness. Never succumb to the mistake of thinking you have to be infallible. Even the kids don't expect that.

Send constant behavioural nudges and cues: correcting or drawing attention to misbehaviour, praising what is good and desired. Above all, keep calm. Showing anxiety or anger is a clear indicator to the students that you are fraying. Convey compete balance and calm – even if inside you are churning like a snow globe.

Stop and reboot the lesson if you need to. That means:

- Getting everyone's attention.

- Getting everyone to stop what they are doing.

- Turn and face you.

- Hands on the desk, no pens held.

- Then deliver a short speech about the behaviour so far.

- Stay calm, reiterate expectations and why they matter.

- Remind them that you expect them to do really well and you hope they will learn.

- Remind them of the consequences of not following directions.

- Never accept rudeness, especially at this point.

- If you have to, have the most difficult student removed to a prearranged parking spot.

And reboot as often as you have to. If you have to do it more than once, make sure that you give out some clear consequences, or students will think you don't mean what you say.

Still my room, my rules

The main problem with cover lessons is that usually the class is unfamiliar with the teacher's expectations, have little or no relationship with them, and therefore don't know where the boundaries are, or how impervious they are.[81]

Cover lessons are much easier if there is a strong 'whole-school culture', and children clearly understand how they should behave in all lessons, not just

---

81   'Perhaps they're made of warm butter?' they wonder. 'Let us discover this together.'

cover lessons. But where the whole-school culture is weak, students behave for *this* teacher or *that* teacher (or not) but not because they are at school. Schools like this frequently have very patchy behaviour throughout. This is why it is important for students to have a relationship with not only their classroom teacher but also the institution of the school. Otherwise, you teach children that it's OK to misbehave with adults they 'don't have a relationship with'.

In a nutshell:

- Make sure you know what the work is in advance. Picking it up as the lesson starts assures that you begin off-balance, and the kids can see it, which sets the tone badly in terms of expectations.

- Have a class list. Being aware of their names is a powerful tool for identifying students. They will then know that they can't simply misbehave and get away with it.

- Get a seating plan, preferably from the regular teacher. Use it. If you're unsure of the names and suspect they're trying it on, check their books and use them as a guide.

- Briefly outline your key expectations. Tell them explicitly that you expect this to be a successful lesson, that you want them to do well, and that you need them to try their hardest. Let them know immediately what your cues are. Many children treat supply lessons as trivial, and one of the major reasons for that is that teachers treat them as disposable.

- Briefly lay out your behaviour expectations with the class. Be positive, but sound like you hope you don't have to follow up on any behaviour. If they don't know you, they probably won't be impressed with a bullying tone, but they need to hear a little steel from you. They need to know you are serious – about them, about the work, about your expectations. Remember: *compassionate consistency.* Your voice should be *warm assertive.*

- Take names when you need to, with a view to following up later. If you don't take names, you will forget who did what.

- Make sure you learn the school behaviour policy if it is a school you are unfamiliar with. You need to let the students know that *you* know the systems, and will use them.

- Also find out the name of who you can call for assistance if you need help, or what the on-call procedure is. Summon help if you need to. The school is (or should be) there to support you.

- Always record misbehaviour and take the time to communicate it to the relevant person. If you can, set and attend sanctions yourself, but make sure no threads are left dangling. The students need to see you mean business, and that might take a few lessons. But once they realise that you are part of the school community and won't give up on them, many of them will start to acknowledge your status, and behave accordingly.

And never, never, accept 'What can you expect? This is a cover lesson.' This attitude bleeds from the teacher's demeanour, and the children pick up on it. Supply lessons are only 'free' lessons because teachers believe them to be, which in turn means the children do too. And the result of that is that even the hardest-working children will do less.

Teach them. It seems odd to even have to say that, but many teachers get into a survival mode: *If I can just last to the end, then I can go home.* In such circumstances, no child will thrive, and no teacher either.

Supply lessons can be a wonderful experience, and they are often a great opportunity to sharpen many skills of teaching and relationships. But without care, they can feel like spending a round in the ring with Mike Tyson. Supply teachers of the world, I salute you.[82]

---

82 Ave Imperator, morituri te salutant! Or possibly 'Ave Imperator, docturi te salutant!'

CHAPTER 14

RAGE AGAINST THE MACHINE: TECHNOLOGY AND BEHAVIOUR

In the closing stages of the first quarter of the 21st century, it may seem strange to talk separately about tech in the classroom, as if it were some new and wonderful thing. Technology is a ubiquitous part of human experience, including education. Technology in the broadest sense has been our servant since the stone age.[83]

But it is important to consider it in the same breath as behaviour, if only because recent decades have provided us with such enormous innovations – smartphones, tablets, the internet, interactive whiteboards and so on – that culture has sometimes struggled to catch and keep up with the pace. One thing that we can be reasonably sure of is that with every wave of technological innovation, someone will claim that from *now* on, everything will be different; *this* technology will change education forever. This has been said since at least the invention of the radio and television, when it was believed that the teacher's role had nearly ended, and lessons would be delivered by screen and speaker. Larry Cuban, who has documented this historical phenomenon, notes that it has been so ubiquitous a claim that he describes it as the 'exhilaration/ scientific credibility/disappointment/teacher-bashing'[84] cycle. The revolution hasn't happened yet.[85]

Mobile phones, the internet, pocket-sized smartphones – these have had an immeasurable impact on how we socialise, hook up, order pizza, argue, and even educate. But we also know that technology has opened up other avenues within education, and that for every opportunity it affords us to innovate or improve how we educate, it also offers problems. Some technologies create new behavioural challenges to the everyday classroom – or reprise old ones – and it is important for every teacher to be aware of these issues in order to address them sensibly.

---

83 Except when we allow it to master us.

84 Cuban, L. (1986) *Teachers and Machines: The Classroom Use of Technology Since 1920*. Teachers College Press. Also: Cuban, L. (2009) *Oversold and Underused: Computers in the Classroom*. Harvard University Press.

85 Although COVID-19 provided an unexpected boost to this model, temporarily.

Smartphones

Smartphones can potentially revolutionise the way we access information. But this revolution comes at a price.

Smartphones are *enormously* distracting. We know that the temptations provided by even the simplest of smartphones proves too much for many students. And why not? That's what they're designed for. They are packed with applications and games designed for one purpose: to occupy our time. Every major social media organisation has teams of behavioural psychologists working on this one dilemma: how to capture the last frontier of real estate: your attention. It's like a modern Yukon Gold Rush. Adults find smartphones hard enough to put down. Is it any wonder that children, lacking many of the skills and resilience of maturity, find it even harder to resist them?

But what is often overlooked is that research strongly suggests that the students for whom this distraction is *most* pronounced are the already disadvantaged students: the behaviourally challenged, the furthest behind academically, or the most impulsive.[86] In other words, the students who need to focus most are the ones most distracted by their siren call.

> We find that mobile phone bans have very different effects on different types of students ... Banning mobile phones improves outcomes for the low-achieving students ... the most, and has no significant impact on high achievers.[87]

This is one reason why teachers must take the challenges they represent seriously: they present an enormous impediment to learning, and threaten to widen the disadvantage gap, if allowed without restriction.

> We find that following a ban on phone use, student test scores improve by 6.41% of a standard deviation. Our results indicate that there are no significant gains in student performance if a ban is not widely complied with. Furthermore, this effect is driven by the most disadvantaged and underachieving pupils. Students in the lowest quartile of prior achievement gain 14.23% of a standard deviation, whilst students in the

---

86   Beland, L. and Murphy, R. (2015) *Ill communication: technology, distraction & student performance*. CEP Discussion Papers (CEPDP1350). Centre for Economic Performance, London School of Economics and Political Science, London, UK.

87   Ibid.

top quartile are neither positively nor negatively affected by a phone ban. The results suggest that low-achieving students are more likely to be distracted by the presence of mobile phones, while high achievers can focus in the classroom regardless of the mobile phone policy.

Smartphones are a problem for learning behaviour, and especially those who struggle the most. It may be true that the most advantaged, most self-disciplined students are relatively unaffected by them, but we do not teach classes entirely composed of such students. It is short-sighted to recommend whole-cohort access to them if we know that it costs the most vulnerable the most. It is irresponsible to advocate their wholesale adoption simply because we might be fortunate enough to teach a small group of highly advantaged children.

Their raison d'etre is to absorb the user's attention. And not in a purposeful or nurturing way – any form of attention will do, and by any means necessary. That means that mobile phones rely on some tried and tested techniques to attract and retain attention:

- Novelty

- Urgency

- Drama

- Pleasure

- Social esteem

This is not to make the case that devices are inherently evil, but to convey the naivety of assuming these devices are harmless. Armies of app designers spend their lives trying to capture your attention long after you have ceased to enjoy giving it. We have all felt the ennui of scrolling through page after page of information that barely pleases us, but we feel too inert to do anything about it, like staring at a television screen after midnight, too lazy to move or go to bed. That doesn't matter to the designers of such apps. As long as you're conscious and staring in the right direction, that's what matters.

But that should concern us enormously as educators. Because the aim of what we do is precisely about:

- Getting children to focus on one thing at a time, not flicking from idea to idea.

- Thinking deeply, not superficially.

- Avoiding distraction.

- Persisting with difficult material.

Social media and entertainment apps encourage the opposite:

- Jumping from thought to thought as quickly and frequently as is *pleasant*

- Thinking lightly and avoiding reflection

- Distractions are the *point*; they are the content

- If material is difficult, move on to something that doesn't trouble your brain.

Again, I stress that there are obviously some excellent uses for smartphones, apps and the opportunities they offer. There are other, better examinations of the utility of such devices, as well as through explorations of the difficulties they present for pedagogy. I will restrict myself to their impact in a strictly behavioural sense.

But even when doing so, it is hard to avoid this conclusion: smartphones (and any device providing independent access to the internet, games-based software or similar) are a huge distraction to children, even when constantly managed. They disproportionately affect the most disadvantaged children, the students already furthest behind, and the children who most need the advantage of a thorough education, socially and academically.

Why does it have such a large impact on the most disadvantaged? On reflection it is obvious: if they already find the work hard, for whatever reason, and they have the option to escape into more pleasant and easier activities, what percentage of students do you think would choose the harder activity over the easier one? Which way does water flow? Would you like to buy this bridge I have for sale?

Even hard-working, committed students find it easy to be tempted to slack off a little when presented frequently or continuously with the opportunity to do so. If students are constantly able to access the internet etc., then we have broken one of our principles: *make behaving easy.*

Presenting your students with a constant diet of temptation to play or slack off is not making it easy to form good habits. It is making it harder. It is obvious that when students have less than ideal habits and willpower, they will be the ones who give in to temptation the most. Hence the effect being disproportionately worse for the most disadvantaged.

No educator should be satisfied with this circumstance. The ones who need the most help are the ones who suffer most from access to smartphones. The Matthew effect takes over.

The Matthew effect revisited

'For to every one who has will more be given, and he will have abundance; but from him who has not, even what he has will be taken away.'[88]

The students that are the furthest behind get further behind. The ones in front find it easiest to stay ahead.

1. Tech should be a useful tool, never used for its own sake

In a very real sense, teachers have been given answers to questions they didn't ask, and solutions to problems that never existed.

Dr Carl Hendrick,
Psyche online magazine[89]

Often the technology we use in classrooms has been driven more by the desire to be innovative than by a sense of what innovations are required. Often it is the doomed desire to spend money until problems go away, and the illusion that the more expensive or novel a thing is, the better it must be. Or crucially, the bigger the educational aim of technology firms, the more they want to sell it, and the more it costs.

---

88 Matthew 25:29, RSV.
89 www.bit.ly/3g3QfxB

Far too frequently in education, we adopt dogma happily and without question. Interactive whiteboards were nowhere, then they were everywhere. iPads sprung into existence, and now schools – *still* – proudly trumpet that their acquisition on a one-to-one basis is the cornerstone of their learning strategy – without any evidence to justify it.[90] And this despite numerous, large-scale examples of such schemes failing spectacularly.[91] Not only does this have an educational implication, it causes a behavioural deficit. How well students behave dictates how well they learn. The behaviours associated with smartphone technology and tablets are often at odds with the ways we learn.

To put it another way, our technology may have revolutionised itself exponentially for the last few decades, but the ways our brains are hard wired to think and behave have not. They remain the same soggy grey sacks of porridge they always have been. Tech, when adopted, should complement the way we think and behave, not attempt to revolutionise it. The brain isn't changing anytime soon. And nor should the essentials of the classroom, or the behavioural expectations you need to make it a safe space.

2. All schools should default to 'no device' policy and then work up from that

Schools and teachers must always justify access to devices for each individual occasion. For any teacher who is building their classroom culture, it is probably wisest to avoid using these attention magnets until you are satisfied that the students will benefit rather than be burdened by them. Their use should be on a case-by-case basis rather than blanket permission. And crucially, one question should always be asked: can this be done better without using tech? Or am I just sprinkling tech on my lesson for the sake of using tech? And if so, why?

Consider the least able, most easily distracted, most in need of school. As with any behavioural routine, always consider the poorly behaved as well as the well behaved. If I am going to use a resource in my classroom (tech or otherwise), how will it land with different children? What do they need to know or be able to do in order to get the benefit from the activity? Are there any possible bear traps I'm walking into e.g. students unable to access or use devices, being tempted to use them badly etc.?

---

90 'Free iPads for nearly 50,000 school pupils in Glasgow (2019) *BBC News Website*, 27th Aug, www.bbc.in/2VsW1iL

91 'The inside story on LA schools' iPad rollout: "a colossal disaster"' (2013) *eSchool News*, 9th Oct, www.bit.ly/33BptHS

Safe behaviour

Using internet-enabled tech also exposes children to numerous safeguarding and safety issues. Bullying; pornography and horror; child-abusers; conspiracy theories and fake news; and so on. While it is possible to obtain a variety of child locks and blocks to minimise these risks, they do not banish them – and besides, most schools and teachers are not tech-savvy enough to manage this perfectly.

Example:

I once set my year 9 class a research activity using computers: they had to find out about the Holocaust, then produce their findings in the form of a poster. They had no great preparation about the topic. The task was designed to provoke their enquiry, creativity, independent investigation and research skills. It was a complete disaster.

Half the class returned posters that stated, sometimes cautiously (*with* question marks) or boldly (without them), that the Holocaust never happened. Some even said it was a conspiracy invented by Zionists. When I asked them what a Zionist was, they were unclear.

It was a disaster of my own creation, because I had expected them to behave like informed adult researchers, when what they were was children. Google took them immediately to the darkest depths of conspiracy and anti-Semitism, and they hoovered it up. I had unconsciously expected them to possess skills of critical thinking they lacked; I tacitly assumed they had background knowledge to underpin that criticality.

This example reminds us that we cannot expect children to demonstrate behaviours or skills they have not been taught.

Example 2:

Police liaison officers in schools tell me that over half their time is spent dealing with cyberbullying and its fallout. Even though children are not supposed to be able join Twitter or Facebook until the age of 13. But unless a parent patrols this, the ambition is often realised.

Through a series of adult/parental failures, we find 12-year-old children lying under their bedsheets at midnight, weeping because a bully's cruelty has reached home and into their most private of spaces, a place where they should be safe and protected. And we allow it; allow the possession of a phone; allow it into a bedroom; allow membership of adult social media communities; and we even pay for all this to happen. The tragedy is that face-to-face bullying still happens, but now it has another, virtual platform in which to operate.

Example 3:

A 13-year-old girl is pressured into sending nude pictures of herself to her 'boyfriend' because 'that's what girlfriends do'. The boy shares them with his friends, and they post them in a public forum. The girl's family eventually move her to another school. The pictures re-emerge from time to time on different forums, forever.

Shouldn't we teach students how to use smart technology rather than banning it?

This is a reasonable point. Two responses:

- That requires an enormous investment of time and effort for a benefit that can be far more easily achieved and maintained by simply restricting access to them. You can teach a dog to ignore a marshmallow on its nose. But the effort and willpower used is enormous. Why bother? Why not just *not* put marshmallows on your dog's nose?[92]

- Teaching children how to use smartphones *is* teaching them how to get used to not having them on all the time, not being available all the time. Children deserve safe spaces free from the need to constantly be online. I call it 'school'.

Children are often habituated (not addicted, although people often conflate these two) from a young age to being online for most of their waking day, to the detriment of anything that requires persistence and focus, e.g. books, thought-provoking cinema, silent reflection and contemplation. The behaviour habit that they need to be taught is 'How not to be online/How to do something else.'

---

92 Traditionally when you use a metaphor like this, some people get very angry. So for the benefit of these people let me reassure you that dogs are not children. You may now go back to laughing at pictures of dogs wearing waistcoats on Facebook. The literal mind cannot comprehend the metaphorical one.

When you are on your phone, you are not where you are. You are not present in the physical space. Your mind is elsewhere.

In order for them to feel that being online is optional rather than normal, they need to be provided with environments where they are not allowed to be online, and to see that as normal too. And that means extended periods away from smartphones.

As adults, how long to do any of us last on our phones before dipping into something pleasant and trivial? And how many times a day do we check our phones needlessly, taking us away from where we are? Studies[93] suggests we check our phones on average 56 times a day, spending three hours and fifteen minutes doing so. If film theatres did not demand phones were packed away, how many theatres would glow with them, as the audience smashed their concentration into a hundred pieces?

Teach them good social media etiquette

Students will have plenty of time to access the internet outside of school. We have no power over how they and their families conduct themselves. But in school, we have a duty of care: to protect and to teach, like the LAPD with elbow patches. And recognising that protection can apply to the virtual world as much as the physical one is an essential part of our behavioural strategy. If they are not safe, they cannot learn as well.

While I am normally the last person to advocate that schools make up for every deficiency in society, in the case of internet safety I am happy to make an exception, because the overwhelming majority of children do not receive a great deal of internet safety advice at home. Most children I have taught were barely aware that Facebook has security settings, giving the lie to the idea of children as 'digital natives' – children are as hapless and helpless a community of consumers as the rest of us. Some of them are tech savvy and some are not.

Some sobering statistics:

- 21% of surveyed girls aged 11 to 18 said they had received a request for a sexual image or message.

---

93 MacKay, J. (2019) 'Screen time stats 2019: Here's how much you use your phone during the workday', www.bit.ly/2JlOcsP

- 4% of surveyed primary school-aged children and 5% of surveyed secondary school-aged children said they had been sent or shown a naked or semi-naked picture or video from an adult.

- 2% of surveyed primary and secondary school-aged children said they had sent a naked or semi-naked picture or video to an adult.

- Less than half (44%) of children aged 12 to 15 said they knew how to change their settings to control who could view their social media.[94]

So part of the school's behavioural curriculum needs to focus on internet safety. There are some great guides already produced that can be downloaded, but in summary:

- Recommend that they should not be on some of the most popular sites unless they are age appropriate and say why. Be honest. Tell them that if you find evidence that they are on any of these sites, parents will be informed.

- Describe to them how to activate the most popular security settings on the most popular sites when they're old enough to access them.

- Tell them what cyberbullying looks like. Many children see it as part of their normal interactions and have to be reminded/taught that it is not normal or appropriate to feel victimised or harassed, even online.

- Teach them about good digital hygiene at home – when they should turn off (at *least* an hour before bed), where they should store the phone (not in the bedroom, for example) and agree time limits to access.

- Be honest and clear about the dangers of sexting, and draw clear boundaries about what is acceptable to send and what isn't. 'Stranger danger' now has to apply to their pockets, backpacks and living rooms.

- Give them numbers of helplines to call if they need anonymous help with any of the above. Give them a way to talk to someone in school about it and let them know that the service is there for them whenever they need it.

---

94   NSPCC (2019) *How safe are our children?*

- And above all, have honest conversations with parents about their part in all of this. It may be difficult to convince a stressed parent to remove a child's phone or delete an app (although not impossible) but agreeing time limits, etiquette etc. at home can be a powerful intervention in a child's wellbeing and mental health.

And in my experience, many, many parents welcome the guidance. Remember the curse of expertise: even if you feel that being safe online is fairly obvious, I can assure you that many do not. And usually, the people who do not think it's obvious are the ones who end up being the victims of ignorance.

The phone proximity effect

Some final thoughts. Studies have shown that merely being in close proximity to a mobile phone can have a significant and measurable impact on student motivation, focus and outcomes, probably due to the fact that students are thinking about looking at it, or what could be happening under its bonnet.[95] So it's not enough to merely tell students not to use them; they need to be out of sight, and as far away as is practically possible. That should mean in a bag on the floor at the very least, and preferably in a locker or similar. Some schools go further and have a system whereby phones are collected and stored at reception, and some schools go further and prohibit them on the premises entirely.

Use the system your school has, but my recommendation is – at minimum – proactively taught behaviour ('We don't want to see the phone at all...') and clearly described consequences ('...or we'll confiscate it...') along with an explanation why ('...because it's a distraction/you don't need it/we want you to succeed and learn, and that means focusing').

Commit to confiscation

Over 95% of schools in the UK have some form of restrictive policy on mobile phones.[96] But often I walk into schools with such policies and still see phones creeping out. Why? Normally it is because they have a confiscation policy but it is not carried out, or not carried out consistently, which is almost as bad. If students know that they might get away with getting their phone out, they'll be

---

95   Ward, A. F., Duke, K., Gneezy, A. and Bos, M. W. (2017) '*Brain Drain: The Mere Presence of One's Own Smartphone Reduces Available Cognitive Capacity*', *Journal of the Association for Consumer Research* 2 (2) pp. 140–154.

96   www.bbc.in/33Fl5Y7

much more tempted to do so. And if a teacher attempts to confiscate it in such circumstances, the bolder student will respond with a gale of protest, pointing out that *Mr Harrison didn't confiscate it yesterday and he's really nice and why are you picking on me?* And so on.

The simple truth is that if students consistently experience confiscation every time a phone appears, then phones stop appearing very quickly. The knowledge that the consequences are uncertain dissolves the deterrence effect.

Thou shall not steal

The classroom teacher should commit to follow the school policy which, if it is sensible, will revolve around confiscation. Even if you yourself don't mind phones in classrooms. Even if you think it's a minor misdemeanour. Even if it's a really nice kid and they were *just checking the time*. It's easy to be laid back in a lesson when things are going well, or when you're trying to get the kids to like you. But it is a synthetic form of a relationship. By currying favour with them, by bending a school rule, you teach them that sometimes they can get away with breaking the rules. You might be OK with that, but you have robbed the authority of the poor teacher next door who is trying their best to get better behaviour in a challenging class but finds it ten times harder because students know teachers are inconsistent. If we are to succeed, we must succeed together, or not at all. We are not tutors working in chambers. We are teachers in a community of teachers and learners. What we do affects everyone. Our behaviour is social too.

How long?

For the consequence to be a deterrent, the students must feel that the confiscation is a real inconvenience rather than merely a mild irritation. Some schools return phones at the next break, which seems more like a valet service than a sanction. Most schools who run successful policies in this area state that the student doesn't receive their phone back until the end of the week; some require that the student's parents or guardians collect it on their behalf, which has a double effect on the child. These kinds of confiscation policies are far more effective a deterrent than a half-hearted removal. Children learn very quickly indeed that if they want to retain their phones – and they do, they do – then they need to make sure they never see daylight in the classroom.[97]

---

97   Like Gremlins, tell your class that they explode in sunshine. Also, don't get them wet.

Only classrooms?

There is a very good argument to be made that this prohibition should extend to all spaces in the school, and I would advocate this. Many schools that have introduced bans in the classroom and beyond have reported positive dividends in outcomes, social skills, and other community benefits.[98] Children in playgrounds allowed access to mobile phones will spend a great deal of their time *not* exercising and *not* talking to one another. If you have any interest in their health or their social skills, one of the best things a school can do is to make sure that public spaces, corridors, playgrounds etc. are similarly safe spaces from tech immersion. Form tutors should also follow this principle, on the understanding that form time is valuable time, not merely an opportunity to catch up on the gossip and take the register.

---

98   www.bit.ly/2JznAo1

CONSISTENCY IS THE FOUNDATION OF ALL HABITS

Practice makes perfect. Perfect practice is better. Habits only last as long they are performed. As soon as we stop practising, we start to lose that habit.

CHAPTER 15
EQUIPMENT

Most students are required to bring something to school, from a show-and-tell, to a pen, to a full set of textbooks, a Bible, a protractor set or a calculator watch.[99] Some schools prescribe tablets; some a ton of sports gear. Whatever they are, they are needed for a reason, presumably because lessons cannot proceed without them. But equipment issues can paralyse a whole class, even if just two or three students find themselves inexplicably lacking. The teacher then spends the next five minutes rooting around for a broken biro in their bag. Worse, unnoticed, the student can miss entire lessons for want of a pair of shoes, or a pencil. Worse still is when a student, devoid of pen, keeps quiet, and the teacher doesn't notice that an hour has gone by with nothing done.

What to do?

The first way to make sure that equipment is routinely brought in is to make equipment routines clear from the outset. Make it explicit what is needed and when. Explain why. Teach them to be self-reliant. Explain where they should get the things they need. Tell them what to do if they are running out. Always indicate that there are avenues of possibility for those who cannot afford their equipment.

This proactive approach should reduce the frequency of 'forgetting'. If we only tell them once what to bring, and if we rely on them remembering after a quick mention in form time, or an assembly, then we have ignored one of our commandments: *make it easy for them to behave*. The ones with better memories, or the ones with more supportive or attentive families, will 'remember' their kit more than the ones who do not possess these advantages. Which means if you rely solely on sanctions and rewards to address this, then you might be doing so unfairly.

The key thing is that you are teaching children to remember. You teach them that equipment is important. For them to learn this, they also need to learn that forgetting equipment has consequences. And that it matters to you.

---

99   The height of status in 1977, I assure you.

Remember that even if the student is facing difficult circumstances, e.g. their parents are divorcing etc., the aim should always be to encourage the student to be able to deal with adversity and maintain good standards. This requires judgement to avoid tipping into either overindulgence or inflexibility. It will always be an act of judgement. If you say to a child that equipment doesn't matter because they have to go to two different homes in a week, then you teach them that it's OK to stop trying. You may not wish to teach them this, but it is the lesson absorbed anyway. You may wish to teach them how to be fully tooled up for school even when it's harder to do so. We don't just teach subjects; we teach students how to be better students and more resourceful people.

And if you do provide equipment to maintain class flow, *always follow up*, otherwise you normalise and enable it. Never forget or treat it as a closed case. Don't allow students to think it doesn't matter. It *does* matter. So show them it does by talking to them about it, making a note for their parents, or asking for an explanation etc. Lessons can be frayed by a stream of students without pens, begging them off you until you have none left, never returning them, and expecting the same the very next lesson. The question is, how many pens do you want to buy? If you get your systems right, it can be zero.

Make the difference between excuses and reasons clear: students may have an excellent reason for not having a pen, but this should not be used as an excuse. Instead, if we teach students to take responsibility, they will learn how to overcome their problems (e.g. ask a peer to loan a pen at the beginning of the day). The caveat is that schools need to make it possible for students to overcome their reasons by building in easy-to-access solutions (e.g. providing tutors with pens to loan out, accompanied by consequences…).

Don't start a war over a pen.[100] Equipment matters, but better to issue a pen and then deal with it after the lesson, maximising lesson flow and learning time, than to have a row that deprives 30 children of an education, replacing it with entertainment. Flow matters in teaching, and disruption punishes everyone. If a student really wants to have a row with you over a pen, then you probably can't fix that in a public space.

But if a student is actively seeking a row over a pen, then you may *need* to remove them; not because you think a pen alone is worth removing a student for, but because there is more at stake: civility in the classroom and the need

---

100 Tbh this is probably good advice without the 'over a pen' clause too.

to be calm and compassionate with one another. These are the things students need to be removed for, not pens. But pens may be the issue over which such things arise. Best to head these problems off at the pass, and stop a little problem becoming a big one.

What can you do?

However, it shouldn't mean that they have to miss out on education as a result. My suggestions are as follows:

- If they forget something simple and small like a pen, supply it – but give out one in a distinctive colour, e.g. purple, so that when you look back over their work you can see how frequently they forgot to bring one. This makes it much easier to discuss the matter at parents' evenings. Just flick through the books and marvel at the purple prose.

- Additionally, you could train them into a state of diminished helplessness. One way to do this is to teach them to bring, for example, three pens to every lesson. 'One to use, one to lose, one to lend,' as I used to say. That way if they do forget one pen, they have a backup and a spare. And if they don't, then their peer may be able to supply one, and this should be a trained expectation.

- Or, make sure that you have a small stock that you can sell, or encourage the school to keep one, if it does not already. This helps to foster another form of independence.

- Teach them to inform you of any deficiencies in their equipment as soon as they enter the classroom, rather than five minutes into the lesson, by which point they are playing catch-up.

- If you have done all of these things, you will minimise disruption caused by lack of equipment. As ever, you will never eliminate it entirely through this method alone. Students also need to see that failing to bring equipment has consequences. This needn't be draconian but should put pressure on the students to remember.

- Record how frequently pens have been forgotten, so it can be tracked.

- Issue a mild sanction for repetition. Mileage will vary with this one, but my preference is that students incur some form of sanction at least after two or three 'forgettings' in a week. You may not wish to pull the trigger on consequences after the first offence, or you may. Remember, patterns of misbehaviour can also trigger complex responses. Investigate why equipment is not coming in. Is there a financial reason? A personal and more difficult reason, such as commuting between two recently estranged parents' homes? A bereavement? Are they being bullied or robbed? Once you establish if there is an abnormal reason for the equipment's absence, you can work out where to go with it.

CHAPTER 16

SEATING PLANS

The architecture of attention, part 1

The teacher should always choose where the students sit.

Because many students value friendship groups over learning, it is highly unlikely that, left to their own devices, students will independently select the seating plan that supports their learning best. It is *extremely* likely that many students will want to sit next to their friends, students they want to be their friends, students they want to harass, and so on. Students' behaviour will be strongly affected by the students that immediately surround them – their immediate audience.

If seated next to close friends, it is more likely that they will chat together. Some students antagonise one another if allowed to be close. Some students show off to one another. Some students will copy other students' behaviour. Seating plans are no trivial thing, and getting it right is not always easy.

The first thing is to start from the default assumption that the seating plan is *your* prerogative. Make sure you have a seating plan in place for all of your classes, apart from exceptional circumstances.

The benefits of a seating plan:

- It encourages students to see the classroom as a learning space, not a social space. It *can* also be social, but on your terms, not theirs.

- It gently but firmly suggests to students that the room is under your supervision and direction, and that the space is governed by structure, boundaries and permissions. This is one reason why it is so important that the teacher insists upon this. It is a first-contact communication: 'My room, my rules.'

- It breaks up friendship groups, which deters unnecessary social chatter.

- It encourages students to make new friends, or to learn how to talk to unfamiliar students.

- It provides respite from students who are forced into close contact with bullies.

- It enables you to split up toxic friendship groups who reinforce one another's misbehaviour.

Suggested principles of a good seating plan:

- Shuffle the deck. Boy/girl/boy/girl is a useful and simple way to randomise the social combinations.

- Alphabetise this in either direction to add a further layer of randomisation.

- Separate students who are known to misbehave together.

- Keep poorly behaved students close to you. This allows greater levels of monitoring, but also means you can assist them with behavioural nudges or support with completing or understanding tasks, a lack of which may form part of their justification for misbehaviour.

- Some commentators emphasise the importance of designing unobstructed walkways through the class, as much as thinking about where the students sit.[101] This makes it easier for a mobile teacher to get around quickly.

Never give in to student requests to allow them to sit together. Ignore protests or promises that they will 'be good' if they sit next to their friends. They *always* say this. But the resolve to stick to this contract often only lasts until the first opportunity to renege on it. If they think that pleading will get them what they want, then they will continue to try it every lesson. So be firm from the start. Don't make promises that you'll think about it if they're good, because every lesson they will ask, 'Have we been good?' in expectation that today will be the day the wall tumbles. And every time you say no, they will scorn you and think you a tyrant, especially if they have been good.

Far better for them to grasp immediately, permanently, that the seating plan is not flexible, and that students are moved only as you will it. Do not let them

---

101 Jones, F. (no date) 'Effective Room Arrangement', *Education World*.
www.bit.ly/3qr3DQU, retrieved 28/06/20

see it as a treat to be moved, because then they will understand that it is a punishment not to be moved. Also you will have taught them that you only move the ones you favour.

Besides, all things being equal, you will have a class of children with varying behaviour patterns. If you allow the 'good' ones to sit with their peers, then you by default leave a pool of 'poorly behaved students' elsewhere. Every mountain creates a valley between itself and its partner.

The only instance where you may allow students to sit with whomever they please (bearing in mind that this is still your reserved privilege) is when you know the whole class to be impeccably behaved, and capable of behaving perfectly well with whomever they sit with. And this will be a rare circumstance indeed.

Adults are often big kids

Consider your experiences with adults in a similar context, e.g. staff training days. In such circumstances, it is common to see staff sitting where they please. In my career, I've visited hundreds of schools and addressed many staff meetings.

And you know how they behave? Very much like the kids.

The most dutiful members of the audience, usually the senior staff, go straight to the front row. All eyes are on them, and woe betide anyone who shirks this. And then all who follow stream into the back row...exactly like students in the class. I watch the hall fill up from the back. I don't blame them. They might feel, like members of a comedy club audience, that people at the front will be expected to participate, or be picked on for answers, more than the ones in the back. And they would probably be right, all things being equal.

Then people start to fill seats, back to front. Rows fill up from the edge, blocking late comers, who are then forced to trudge to the front, where they sit, helpless and unhappy.

And when we begin, what happens then? If in tables, and a task is set, then frequently this: some members of the staff fall upon the task with gusto. If there is sugar paper and pens, one person will either race to be in charge of it, or have to be assigned scribing responsibilities like a death sentence. Someone will draw something completely unrelated. Some of them will be on their phones, discreetly or not; some of them will completely task-avoid; some of them will chip off to the toilet the instant the task begins ('I'm just getting some photocopying'). Task sharing becomes dramatically unequal, and it shows.

And if this is what we get from professionals who are there as part of their salaried employment (and presumably under the watchful eye of their line managers), then can we expect children to behave any better? Should we be amazed that they do worse, given their relative differences in maturity, intellectual and social development, and paralysing interest in the opinion of others?

No. So seating plans are the best way of short-circuiting this problem.

Make learning as easy as possible

Why let them choose their chair? The temptation to misbehave becomes so high. Nobody should design a class that puts distractions in their way.[102]

Yet we often feel under great pressure to do so. Why? The reason I most commonly hear cited is 'to allow them to develop socially'. But what evidence is there that this is a way of developing their social skills as opposed to simply allowing them to socialise with exactly the same students they would socialise with outside of the classroom? What has been added?

Nothing useful. But what has been added is the temptation to *not* do the work directed, and to do less of it when they do. This is not a help but a hindrance to them, and we should be mindful that everything we do is to their benefit. If you want them to learn in groups, or to develop positive social skills, teach them. Don't expect them to pick them up by osmosis. Some might, but many won't. Why would children flourish in such an erratic and chaotic environment? It is an abdication of the teacher's adult responsibility not to provide them with the most nurturing and structured space we can.

Rows, columns, islands, horseshoes, or hedgehogs?

Commonly, seating plans are often dominated by an ideology that assumes children work best collaboratively, that learning is an activity best facilitated by

---

102 But they still do. I've seen several school rebuilds where architects (usually not teachers) breathlessly designed classrooms that were open-plan, or made out of odd mezzanine levels, or with the teacher in the round, and worse. Schools then spend their tiny maintenance budgets trying to fix this, forever. I've even seen schools *ask* for such features, then self-immolate in buyer's regret. These are the mistakes we make when we allow our idealism and ideology to obstruct the practicalities of the classroom.

group work. This is represented in the classroom by tables bundled together so that students work in little platoons of four or five. This model is stronger the lower down the age range you look, until by the very early years it assumes the unquestionable quality of dogma.

Unfortunately there isn't a lot of evidence to suggest that it actually helps learning in the way people often claim. There seems to be little obvious benefit in children being made to work in groups by default. What frequently happens, of course, is that children don't work in groups, but work individually at the same table, which seems to defeat the point.

So if there's no evidence of a learning boost by this seating plan, what are the more explicit behavioural implications?

Seating plans based on groups immediately present us with one very clear and obvious challenge: students find other students fascinating. Peers represent distraction, interest, entertainment, communication, an audience, a sounding board, and all the delights that society provides. Contrast that with what the teacher may be offering. Learning, however exciting, can be hard work. It might even feel difficult in the moment. It may take focus, concentration, and sustained effort to coax the genie of joy out of its dark lamp.

But within arm's length, there are faces to look at, ears and eyes to catch. Jeremy Bentham, the utilitarian philosopher, proposed a simple equation that dominated how we make decisions, which he called the *hedonic calculus*. When faced with two competing choices, we look at each option and quickly work out how much pain or pleasure each one entails. Then we put them both on a set of mental scales, and the one that is heaviest with fun wins, and we run with that. For many children, the answer to the hedonic calculus of 'hard maths' versus 'jokes with Ryan' represents a gravity too great to escape.

Of course, this effect is not spread evenly among the class. Some students are more than capable of paying attention even when surrounded by temptation. Some are, but not at all, and some are somewhere in the middle. We should expect this spectrum. But what we realise is that we have – by design – provided students with an environment where some will struggle more than others to focus on what is being said or discussed. The teacher will find that they have to do more work correcting behaviour or reminding these students to focus. The most able will be fine; the least able fall furthest behind.

The architecture of attention, part 2

If your priority is to maximise the environment for focus and attention, one simple and easy solution is to sit students in rows and columns, either at individual desks, or more frequently with a shoulder partner at the same desk. This creates an attention architecture where the gaze (and therefore focus) defaults to the front, and the teaching zone. And crucially, it leans away from the eyes and faces of others.

But what about group work?

Nothing could be simpler; ask (or rather teach) students to turn quickly round to their peers behind, and with their shoulder partners, a group of four forms easily. And equally, this group can be dissolved just by turning back. Best of all, the default is still forward-facing and teacher-focused. While this paradigm may challenge the thinking of some teachers, particularly those of younger children, it is the most flexible and, to my mind, most just way to ensure that children are supported with their learning. They still have peers on the same desk for shoulder conversations, or at the very most, a foot away at the next desk. They are hardly isolated. So, it enjoys the best of both worlds: instant access to peers when needed; instant access to a boundaried, personal learning space when required. The reverse is not true; tables in groups lack this flexibility.

Research in this area is not conclusive, but indicative. It suggests that rows improve on-task behaviour for individual work, and appear to decrease on-task behaviour for collaborative work.[103] So if you are interested in improving behaviour, you might also need to consider what kind of activities your students will be doing predominantly. If individual, use rows; if group work, use tables. Intuition would probably guess as much (but it is always useful to have our intuitions challenged or confirmed by evidence bases). This means that if you teach the very young child, and most of your activities are collaborative, table islands make sense. If you want them to work predominantly in ones and twos, rows work best.

Inclusion, equity, and the seating plan

'Evidence supports the idea that students display higher levels of appropriate behaviour during individual tasks when they are seated in rows, with disruptive students benefiting the most.'[104]

---

103 Wannarka, R. and Ruhl, K. (2008) 'Seating arrangements that promote positive academic and behavioural outcomes: a review of empirical research', *Support for Learning* 23 (2).
104 Ibid.

That last phrase deserves careful consideration. If we are interested in inclusion, equity, and providing the most help to those who need it, to the already disadvantaged and under-privileged, then shouldn't we build seating plan models that commit to those aspirations? Who are we really helping – and hindering – the most when we choose to build islands or horseshoes?

Row and column seating models can be manipulated into group-friendly shapes far more easily than table islands can be engineered into individual spaces. A second argument could be the growing body of evidence which suggests that group work is often not a useful or efficient vehicle for a good deal of learning. Teachers must consider how they balance their desire for children to interact and learn social skills, with their desire for children to learn the content of the curriculum, and to what extent these aims can be achieved simultaneously, or by discrete activities.

A last word: many classrooms are laid out not by teachers, but by premises managers, superintendents, or architects. I have sat in on meetings with new school designers as they discussed how to maximise student capacity within a given space and I have watched as they confidently assumed that this factor was the only question of any relevance. This then led to designs that required horseshoe seating patterns that necessarily create an odd island community buried inside the embrace of its arms. But these considerations are peripheral to the needs of the teacher, and more importantly the student. Who is the classroom being designed for: the designer or the user?

Knights of the Round Table

Ultimately, the design of the classroom is only one factor among many that affect behaviour. If behaviour is impeccable, then the shape doesn't matter, and you can have them in a human pyramid on motorbikes, juggling medicine balls. If students are all equally keen, motivated, self-disciplined and capable, you can overcome any temptation.

But not many teachers have classes like that. Most of us teach human beings. The marshmallow test is one of the most famous experiments in social science research. It examined if children could resist present temptation in exchange for future reward, and how this correlated with later-life success. Children were given a marshmallow and told that if they could avoid eating it for 15 minutes, they would get another one, but not if they ate it. Much was made of the result, but more recently, experiments have suggested that social factors, not willpower, may contribute more to improved outcomes later in life.

For the purposes of the classroom, I hold it as highly probable that students who are better at regulating their behaviour will learn more efficiently than those who cannot. Whether this leads directly to improved earnings or university placements is for others to decide. Social factors cannot be ignored, but it would be equally as foolish to ignore personal ones. And social factors are the ones we can least directly influence as educators, and personal endeavour the most. [105]

Teachers should be free to decide the seating plan model that best suits the aims of the classroom, but it is important for us to be sure what those aims actually are, in order for us to consider what tools we need to achieve them.

---

105 Mischel, W. and Ebbesen, E. B. (1970) 'Attention in delay of gratification', *Journal of Personality and Social Psychology.*

CHAPTER 17
RECORDS

We spend a lot of time worrying about how to get students to remember things. We need to spend some time asking how we can make sure that *we* remember things too.

Memories are *short*. The Ebbinghaus forgetting curve (below),[106] one of the most reliable findings from cognitive psychology, suggests that we lose around half of our learning within days or weeks of encountering it, unless it is somehow consolidated and secured. The rate at which we forget material depends on several factors, such as the difficulty of the material, how meaningful it was to us, stress levels, sleep poverty etc.

Memories are also highly *fallible*. Our brains are not perfect photocopiers of our experiences. We interpret; we filter things out (and in); we remember things that are useful, or shocking, or interesting, or meaningful to us, or that support our existing beliefs. We temporarily forget memories, and then, remembering them, think they are new (*cryptomnesia*). Even eyewitness recollections of crime scenes have been found to often be unreliable.[107]

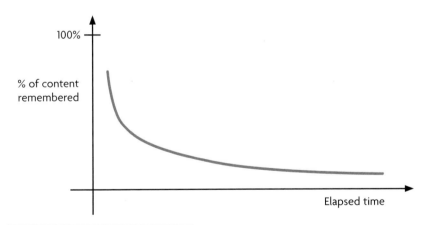

106 Ebbinghaus, H. (1913) *Memory: A contribution to experimental psychology.* (H. A. Ruger and C. E. Bussenius, trans.) Teachers College Press
107 Arkowitz, H. and Lillienfeld, S. O. (2010) 'Why Science Tells Us Not to Rely on Eyewitness Accounts', *Scientific American Mind*, Jan.

We often have a false confidence in how much we remember. We reassure ourselves that we won't forget 'this' fact, 'this' phrase, 'this' number sequence. But then we do – even important things. Our brains are ruthless cleaners, tidying up our memories and exterminating all but the most essential things. We are drenched in sensation every minute we are alive, and our conscious mind is constantly full to the brim with input. We simply cannot hold it all in at the same level of clarity and awareness and focus. The mind constantly burns old memories on a bonfire of utility, novelty and schema.

Our memories are also *tricksters*. Remembering things is often hard. Recognising this labour, we have developed tools and strategies to outsource our memory. It resulted in one of the greatest inventions since civilization began, one which could be seen as a prerequisite for civilisations to develop past the Stone Age: writing.

Without it, every generation is doomed to forget everything apart from what can be memorised in a web of oral histories. With it, we accumulate pebbles of wisdom and knowledge every generation, adding to the mountain year by year. Our experience becomes a ocean of billions of memories, into which we dip and hold our handful.

And this applies to classrooms too. Teachers choke with input, flowing from all directions all day long. Students are agents of chaos as much as order. Sixty minutes with thirty people will present you with more experience than can be remembered by a hundred cameras and microphones.

You know nothing

Because of this, it is incredibly easy for teachers to forget even important things that have happened in a lesson or school day. Which means that when parents' evening comes around, and someone asks you how Ryan is doing, you often find you can give the vaguest of responses. 'He's doing fine,' you say, struggling for detail that's lost, like tears in rain.[108] That's not good enough.

So write things down as much as possible. That doesn't mean a diary of every minute – just the minutes that matter. And no novels – just a note taken somewhere in order for you to follow up later, or to use that data usefully.

---

108 Most teachers have seen things you people wouldn't believe.

We don't write things down to remember them. We write them down so we can *forget*. So we can forget and clear our minds to think about what we need to think about *now*. Then, we return to the written record and remember when it needs to be remembered. Then we forget about it again. It is a constant spring clean of the mind, and it is liberating. People who keep lists are happy people,[109] because they are no longer paralysed by trying to keep everything in their heads, and the creeping dread of the certain knowledge that something has been forgotten, something has been missed, something *important*.

So, every lesson, write down things you need to remember, such as:

- Absences

- Lateness

- Failure to bring equipment

- Acts of rudeness

- Acts of noteworthy kindness

- Low effort

And so on. Some teacher planners have convenient boxes you can label and tick as a fast way to record effort, homework etc.

Record all significant behaviour issues at a local level (in your planner/diary) and also at the whole-school level (using SIMS, Bromcom etc.). Your school probably has a whole-school data record system. Use it. It is in your interest to get used to it so that you no longer fear it or find it more of a burden than it needs to be. If you avoid using it, you will forever be a stranger to its intricacies, and simple tasks will feel like mammoth ones and crucially, you won't want to use it…which becomes a vicious circle. So use it, little and often.

Write as briefly as possible. But always prioritise the record of important specifics of misbehaviour so that they can be recalled with detail when they need to be. In a parents' evening, or a meeting with a line manager, or a student or a mentor, it isn't enough to say, 'Ryan was rude to me,' because you forgot

---

109 Survey sample: 1000 people who keep lists.

what was said. Listeners will assume 'rudeness' means what they want to assume. Often people can think it means 'He rolled his eyes at me.' But if you say, 'Ryan said, "Go fuck yourself, you silly bitch,"'[110] then that carries a little more impact. Details matter, especially grisly ones.

When I used to run a club, we would occasionally receive noise complaints from local residents who believed that when they moved into the West End party zone of London, they had somehow moved into a quiet, sleepy garden village for retirees. The best advice I had from our lawyers was to record *everything*, there and then, before we went home. So if a resident called us up at 3 a.m. and told us to turn that damn racket down, we could write down the time, the place, and the conversation we had, along with relevant context. On one memorable occasion, the club had been shut for an hour when someone complained that the music was so loud, his walls were shaking. This information proved to be much more useful in subsequent licence hearings than, 'He's called a few times, but it was Gregorian chant night' or something.

Knowledge is power, as Francis Bacon observed. Restorative conversations, meetings with parents, with managers, are all made more efficient by accurate and relevant detail. Guessing isn't enough.

Big data and real people

Also, good data means that you can spot patterns of misbehaviour over time, which might lead to a better understanding of how to resolve it. I once taught a girl who was late for school every Monday and Tuesday, but only an examination of her attendance sheet revealed the pattern. When we probed it, we discovered she had two disabled parents to take care of on those mornings only. So, a workaround was created (she was granted late entry privileges) rather than simply reacting to the behaviour as a series of solitary and unconnected events (and doing the wrong thing, e.g. setting a sanction).

When you sit down with a student and talk to them about their behaviour, avoid *he said/she said* tug-of-wars by referring to your notes, bristling with information. If you say to a student, 'Your behaviour needs to improve,' then don't expect to get too far if you can't be specific. It's too easy for them to simply say, 'No it doesn't. I behave really well.'

---

110 A magic moment that happened to me.

People are great at self-justification. We're not so bad, it wasn't our fault, the teacher is picking on me, I didn't mean it, etc. But if you can say to a student, 'You've been late for half of your lessons this term. You've been sent out once a week on average. You've had 100 detentions. You've not had a pen for three weeks and a day…' etc., then you have a case they have to consider.

Or not. But at least you have a case. It shows that you aren't just picking on them, that you aren't just imagining it, and that maybe – maybe – there is something here they have to address.

Also, this kind of data is invaluable when it comes to persuading parents that their child's behaviour may not be the same as it is at home. I have lost count of the number of times I have had to persuade parents that their child's version of events may not be definitive and comprehensive.

Let me be clear: everyone lies.[111] Some people almost never lie, and some people almost always do, and most people lie somewhere in between. But everyone lies. I've seen the sweetest kids lie blind to their parents. The reasons are usually obvious: the fear of sanction, not wanting their disapproval, an attempt to get the teacher in trouble, and so on. All the reasons why people might lie are the same reasons why children might also lie. I've seen kids lie about starting small fires, and when confronted with video evidence of them doing so, will look you in the eye and say deadpan, 'Nope.' Or my favourite, 'I don't know how that person looks so much like me, but it can't be me because I didn't do it.'

There's no faulting that logic.

Summary:

- *Analyse the patterns to find out your hotspots and causes for concern.*

- *Evidence is king when following up.*

---

111 House, Gregory, *House*, Heel and Toe Productions.

EVERYONE WANTS TO MATTER

The need to matter, to be valued, to form sincere relationships with others, is at the heart of being human. Students need to know they can find these in their education, or they will seek them elsewhere.

CHAPTER 18
REBOOTING

A question that teachers frequently ask is, 'I've had my students for some time now, but behaviour isn't where I want it. Is it too late to reboot the expectations?'

The answer is, happily, no, it is never too late. A classroom culture can be rebooted at any time in your relationship with your students. But it requires strategy, nerve and determination. It is rarely as simple as simply reminding them of the rules. It resembles a computer that has frozen or fails to respond in some way. It can require a *soft* or a *hard* reboot.

Often behaviour slides because of:

- A failure to administer consequences reliably or routinely.

- Saying one thing but doing another.

- Failing to challenge poor norms.

- Accepting pushback.

- Allowing students to rewrite the norms.

The soft reboot

Sometimes, students have forgotten what the core routines and norms of the classroom are. This might be because you have failed to remind them often enough, or sincerely enough. You may have started to allow some things that you would never have done before. You may have been lulled into a false sense of security – behaviour may have been good for a while. You may have forgotten what you wanted from them in the first place. Your goal posts may have shifted, and you may now convey different expectations than before.

This is often very hard for a teacher to notice. Things change slowly, like hair growing, or weight around a waistline, until one day clothes no longer fit, and you wonder where the gymnast went and why you suddenly seem to have a body like a dropped lasagne.[112]

---

112 Boyle, F. (2016) Feb 19th, The Apollo Theatre, London.

This is why it is very important for teachers to be super-noticers of such things, and to have systems in place that discern when standards are slipping or failing to find purchase. Normally this means having explicit standards that are publicly communicated and capable of being verbalised or checked in some way. That way, it becomes easier to discern when they have been explicitly transgressed.

But if the standards are purely a mental exercise, and forever blurred or ambiguous, it becomes harder to tell if the lines have been crossed. To put it another way, if you want to know if you've gained weight, weigh yourself. Weighing isn't the end of the process. But it is an essential part of it. I have often heard 'You don't fatten a pig by weighing it.' Which is trivially true, but useless advice, because you don't know if a pig is getting fatter or thinner, or needs more or less feed, without weighing it. That's what weighing is for, not to make it fat. To find out if things are changed and what you need to do in order to respond to it.

Students are sometimes useful for telling you if your standards have slipped – *if* you ask the right ones. They're usually pretty blunt too – *You're not as strict as you used to be,* or *You let us get away with stuff you never did before,* for example. Feedback is a gift.[113] Ask the *right* kids though – normally the best-behaved children, who often have the most sensible opinions on such things.

I'd probably not ask the worst behaved children, at least not early in your relationship with them, because frequently kids who find it hard to self-regulate aren't great at helping you develop complex classroom systems.[114] I've watched and cringed in horror as new, keen teachers have exposed themselves to whole-class, 360-degree feedback sessions that resembled struggle sessions in Mao's China. That's a brutal thing to do to yourself, and best avoided. Novices are not experts, so why should we assume expertise? It can potentially offer perspective, but that isn't the same thing.

So, we assume that things have slid, or you've never managed to reach the heights towards which you aspired in the first place. What then?

The soft reboot is the simplest way to move things forward. It assumes that your class is reasonably biddable, knows the systems reasonably well, but is sporadically poorly behaved, or erratic in their habits. If this is the case, then soft reboot like this:

---

113 But always ask for the receipts.
114 Fancy that.

Ctrl + Alt + Del

Start your very next lesson. Stand in front of your students and instead of diving straight into whatever task or work you normally would, wait for their attention and then focus the first ten minutes of the lesson on behaviour. You could use a script to do so. It should contain the following beats:

- Some of the learning has been terrific, and some of the behaviour has too.

- Some of the behaviour is holding back how we learn, some people are losing out, and some people aren't being treated with dignity.

- I want things to be better and I want things to be better for you and for all of us.

- When we succeed, we succeed together. When we do well, we all do well.

- Here's what we need to focus on.

If you sell the reboot like this, then it's rare for any student to object.

- You could clarify what the routines and norms are.

- You could give examples of what that might look like in practice.

- You should be clear about specific behaviours that you do not want to see again.

- You should reiterate not just what the consequences are, but what behaviours are desirable, and why.

- You should also reiterate the consequences.

- You *could* get students to suggest ways things could be better (of course, only accepting the ones you agree with, and steering their views round to that understanding). But it's probably safer to assume responsibility and simply tell them what needs to happen. Otherwise they may simply try to shift all responsibility onto the teacher, or suggest inappropriate pseudo-improvements.

This is the beginning of the reboot. It must be delivered with sincerity, and with the understanding that things will only get better if *everyone* tries hard to do better. And this includes the teacher. This usually means committing to:

- Noticing more.

- Challenging students more.

- Setting more consequences.

- Being more consistent.

- Following up.

- Using the system as a blueprint, not a serving suggestion.

- Checking that you are sticking to your new standards and boundaries.

If things slide again (and they may), reboot again. Persistence is what pays off. Giving up causes the reboot to fade away like mist. This where your mindset is vital, where your head must be totally in the game in order to succeed. You must wear down their resolve to misbehave by presenting them with an adamantine resolve of your own not to back down.

Or you may need a *hard reboot*.

The hard reboot
Turning it on and off again at the mains

This is when behaviour has deteriorated to such an extent that the norms have not so much slid as collapsed in an avalanche. The hard reboot resembles the soft reboot, but with the following bolt-ons:

- Take time to examine not just their ways, but *your* ways. Be honest. Have you given up? Do you let things go?

- Look at the greater school structure. Has anything changed? Is it supportive? Have personnel changed, with accompanying changes in follow-up?

- Be ten times clearer.

- Be brutally honest.

- Take much longer to explain and reiterate the seriousness of the behaviour issue, and what they should do to get better. Actively make them practice the norms and routines, not just tell them. Revert to 'teach them' mode.

- Subsequent to the hard reboot, be much more resolute in how efficiently you administer consequences. Let the class see that you mean business. Reprimand, retain, remove if needs be. Don't accept rudeness – towards you especially, but anyone in the class. Students often see failure to remove abusive children from lessons as a sign that you're fine with it. Persistent misbehaviour must be challenged, both verbally inside the lesson, and punitively and pastorally outside of it. Failure to do so also indicates to the students that their behaviour wasn't so bad, or no big deal. You have normalised it by not taking action.

- Always be warm/assertive in your toner and demeanour. But never sacrifice assertive for warm. They need to be led out of the mess.

The follow-up must be much more exacting and *will* test you. The class will try to steer you back to the old norms. Cultures resist change. For every action, there is an equal and opposite reaction. Inertia is a powerful factor in human nature, and people frequently prefer a familiar, comfortable but negative custom to a new, positive one. Let them get used to the 'new new,' the new normal.

Inertia may be powerful, but so is momentum. When students start to see the behavioural weather changing around them, many will be inspired by it, and find better reasons to follow suit. Norms beget norms. If enough pressure is applied, water can flow backwards, but the energy will have to come initially from you. Once it starts to flow, students will start to self-maintain their customs to some extent.

But you will never, never be able to relax and stop investing your energy and focus on these matters. Entropy, to carry on with the physics metaphor, is the natural state towards which we all travel. Creation takes far more effort than destruction, and teaching and learning is one of the most useful acts of creation there is. And that's why all the effort is worth it.

MY ROOM, MY RULES

The teacher is the authority in the classroom. This authority is rooted in necessity, compassion, and efficiency. Children need an adult. The teacher's power entails great responsibility.

FINAL THOUGHTS

The candle in the wind

In 1958, T.H. White published his masterpiece, *The Once and Future King*. Like Ursula K. Le Guin, 'I have laughed at his great Arthurian novel and cried over it and loved it all my life.' It mesmerised me as a child, and mesmerises me still, each re-reading unpicking a new layer of meaning and insight.

Throughout the books, King Arthur fights in vain to maintain peace in his kingdom. But no matter what he does, no matter how clever his strategies, war inevitably erupts again. The book ends exactly where it began, in chaos and fighting. But in between, he builds Camelot, a place and a time of peace, where the monsters are slain and people are ruled by law, not might-makes-right, at least for a while.

Arthur, miserable and alone at the end of his life, in his tent, preparing for the final battle between himself and the armies of his son Mordred, considers his life to have been a failure. He united the warring tribes of England by conquest and brought peace. He overturned the aristocratic law of the jungle by creating the Round Table, through which violence could be channelled into chivalry. And he pre-empted *Magna Carta* by chaining everyone – even kings – to law. To no avail. Humanity seemed to tilt almost by instinct into conflict and blood.

In *T.H. White: Letters to a Friend*, Francois Gallix writes, 'The purpose of the books... ... [was] the search for an antidote to war.' And in this, perhaps Arthur (and White) was only partially successful. But he was most successful not just when he stopped people fighting, but when he created peace, and the conditions where peace was more likely. Because you can never *destroy* war; you can only shackle it. You can never end the factors that lead to war, because they are buried in human nature; you divert their energies into peace.

And you can never stop doing this, because as long as people remain people with differing values and limited resources, we will experience conflict. Therefore our commitment to peace must be equally unceasing. If it seems depressingly inevitable that this means war will always break out again eventually, I can only say that its minimisation, and the creation of as much peace as possible, seems as noble as any quest that any knight ever rode on.

So too in classrooms. Students will never be perfectly biddable or good. Classrooms will never automatically form into manicured gardens of calm and diplomacy. These are acts of constant construction, like songs. They exist as long as we create them.

We should not count as failure our inability to create and achieve perfection, forever, as if it were an achievable state. We attribute success to those moments when we are successful, whether that be a decade, a day or a millennium. Peace, however fleeting, is always a victory, and searching for the Holy Grail of calm, safe spaces where all children can flourish is never a failure until we give up trying. And the beautiful truth is that with patience, wit and persistence, we can build better classrooms for all children where learning and wisdom and civility are more likely, and more common than not.

That is something worth fighting for. I hope this book plays a part, however small, in your ability and resolve to do so. The candle is yours to look after, and its light yours to share.

Rex quondam, Rexque futurus.

Tom Bennett
The Ford of Rom
2020

FURTHER READING

Teach Like a Champion, Doug Lemov

Why Don't Students Like School?, Daniel Willingham

What Every Teacher Needs to Know about Psychology, David Didau and Nick Rose

The Craft of the Classroom, Michael Marland

These four books are the simplest and most useful guides to behaviour I have come across. Because time is not infinite, you can only devote so much of it to any one area. If you are a teacher, or are involved in working with students, I suggest these books as a priority. Starting with Lemov's classic, then Willingham, then Rose/Didau, then Marland.

And to aid digestion, one more: Bill Rogers, *Classroom Behaviour*.

FURTHER READING

BIBLIOGRAPHY

Ashman, G. (2018) *The truth about teaching: an evidence-informed guide for new teachers.* Sage Publication Ltd.

Aurelius, M. (2004) *Meditations.* Penguin Books.

Birbalsingh, K, (2016) *Battle hymn of the tiger teachers.* Woodbridge: John Catt Educational.

Birbalsingh, K. (2020) *Michaela: the power of culture.* Woodbridge: John Catt Educational.

Boethius (1969) *The consolations of philosophy.* Penguin Classics.

Boland, E. (2016) *The battle for room 314: my year of hope and despair in a New York City high school.* New York City: Grand Central Publishing.

Boxer, A. (2019) *The researchED guide to explicit and direct instruction.* Woodbridge: John Catt Educational.

Brower, F. (2019) *100 ideas for primary teachers: supporting pupils with autism.* Bloomsbury.

Bruyckere, P. de (2018) *The ingredients for great teaching.*

Bruyckere, P. de, Kirschner, P. and Hulshof, C. (2015) *Urban myths about learning and education.*

Carr, A. (1995) *The only way to stop smoking.* Penguin Books.

Carrithers, M. (1992) *Why humans have cultures: explaining anthropology and social diversity.* OUP.

Caviglioli, O. (2019) *Dual coding with teachers.* Woodbridge: John Catt Educational.

Chalk, F. (2011) *It's your time you're wasting.* Monday Books.

Chenoweth, K. (2017) *Schools that succeed: how educators marshal the powers of systems for improvement.* Harvard Education Press.

Christodoulou, D. (2014) *Seven myths about education.* Routledge.

Cialdini, R. B. (2016) *Influence: the psychology of persuasion.* Collins.

Cordasco, F. (1987) *A brief history of education.* Littlefield, Adams & Co.

Davies, W. T. and Shepherd, T. B. (1949) *Teaching: begin here.* London: Epworth Press.

Didau, D. and Rose, N. (2016) What every teacher needs to know about psychology. Woodbridge: John Catt Educational.

Dinham, S. (2016) *Leading learning and teaching.* ACER.

Dixon, P. (2019) *Rhetoric.* Routledge.

Donnelly, K. (20019) *Australia's reading revolution.* Connor Court Publishing.

Egan, K. (2004) *Getting it wrong from the beginning: our progressivist inheritance from Herbert Spencer, John Dewey and Jean Piaget.* New Haven, CT: Yale University Press.

Elliott, J., Hufton, N.R., Willis, W. and Illushin, L. (2005) *Motivation, engagement and educational performance: international perspectives on the contexts for learning.* 10.1057/9780230509795.

Fleming, T. J. (2016) *Ben Franklin: inventing America.* Voyageur Press.

Garelick, B. (2016) *Maths education in the US: still crazy after all these years.* Modern Educator Press.

Gill, A. A. (2018) *The best of A. A. Gill.* W&D.

Goddard, V. (2014) *The best job in the world.* Independent Thinking Press.

Halpern, D. (2015) *Inside the nudge unit: how small changes can make a big difference.* WH Allen.

Hattie, J. (2012) *Visible learning for teachers.* Routledge.

Hawkes, H. (2009) *Autism: a parent's guide.* Need2Know.

Haydn, T. (2007) *Managing pupil behaviour: improving the classroom atmosphere.* Routledge.

Hendrick, C., Macpherson, R. and Caviglioli, O. (2019) *What does this look like in the classroom? Bridging the gap between research and practice.* Woodbridge: John Catt Educational.

Hess, F. M. (2013) *Cage-busting leadership.* Cambridge, MA: Harvard Education Press.

Hirsch, E. D. (2006) *The knowledge deficit: closing the shocking education gap for American children.* Houghton Mifflin.

Hirsch, E. D., Kett, J. F. and Trefil, J. (1988) *Cultural literacy: what every American needs to know.* New York: Vintage Books.

Howard, K. (2020) *Stop talking about wellbeing: a pragmatic approach to teacher workload.* Woodbridge: John Catt Educational.

Hughes, T. (1993) *Tom Brown's schooldays.* Wordsworth Classics.

Jones, K. (2010) *Education in Britain: 1944 to the present.* Polity Press.

Kalenze, E. (2019) *What the academy taught us.* Woodbridge: John Catt Educational.

Kirschner, P. A. and Hendrick, C. (2020) *How learning happens.* London: Routledge.

Lemov, D. (2010) *Teach like a champion: 49 techniques that put students on the path to college.* San Francisco: Jossey-Bass.

Lemov, D., Woolway, E. and Yezzi, K. (2012) *Practice perfect : 42 rules for getting better at getting better.* San Francisco: Jossey-Bass.

Leslie, I. (2014) *Curious: the desire to know why and why your future depends on it.* Quercus.

Marland, M. (1993) *The craft of the classroom.* Heinemann Educational Publishers.

Martin, P. R. and Bateson, P. (2007) *Measuring behaviour: an introductory guide.* Cambridge: Cambridge University Press.

Marzano, R., Marzano, J. S. and Pickering, D. (2003) *Classroom management that works: research-based strategies for every teacher.* Alexandria, VA: Association for Supervision and Curriculum Development.

Maslow, A. (1943) 'A theory of human motivation', *Psychological Review.* 50. 370–396.

McCourt, M. (2019) *Teaching for mastery.* Woodbridge: John Catt Educational.

Mccrea, P. (2019) *Memorable teaching: leveraging memory to build deep and durable learning in the classroom.* Woodbridge: John Catt Educational.

McGuinness, D. (1997) *Why our children can't read and what we can do about it: a scientific revolution in reading.* Free Press.

Meyer, E. (2015) *The culture map.* Public Affairs.

Miller, A. (1996) *Pupil behaviour and teacher culture.* London: Cassell.

Moore, A. (1987) *Watchmen.* Titan Books.

Morris, D. (1969) *The naked ape.* Corgi Books.

Murphy, J. (2019) *The researchED guide to literacy.* Woodbridge: John Catt Educational.

Nutt, J. (2020) *Teaching English for the real world.* Woodbridge: John Catt Educational.

Paul, A. M. (2004) *The cult of personality: how personality tests are leading us to miseducate our children, mismanage our companies, and misunderstand ourselves.* New York: Free Press.

Peal, R. (2014) *Progressively worse: the burden of bad ideas in British schools.* Civitas.

Peterson, K. D. and Deal, T. (2009) *The shaping school culture field book.* Jossey-Bass.

Pink, D. H (2009) *Drive: the surprising truth about what motivates us.* New York, NY: Riverhead Books.

Pondiscio, R. (2019) *How the other half learns.* Avery.

Postman, N. (1987) *Amusing ourselves to death.* Metheun.

Ravitch, D. (2000) *Left back: a century of battles over school reform.* Touchstone.

Rees, T. (2018) *Wholesome leadership.* Woodbridge: John Catt Educational.

Ritchie, S. (2016) *Intelligence: all that matters.* London: Hodder and Stoughton.

Rogers, B. (2011) *Classroom behaviour: a practical guide to effective teaching, behaviour management and colleague support.* London: SAGE.

Rousseau, J. (1988) *The social contract and discourses.* Everyman.

Sapolsky, R. M. (2018) *Behave: the biology of humans at our best and worst.* Penguin Random House.

Scruton, R. (2016) *Confessions of a heretic.* Notting Hill Editions.

Seidenberg, M. (2017) *Language at the speed of sight: how we read, why so many can't, and what can be done about it.* Basic Books.

Shaw, J. (2019) *Making evil: the science behind humanity's dark side.* Canongate.

Sherrington, T. and Caviglioli, O. (2020) *Teaching walkthrus.* Woodbridge: John Catt Educational.

Skinner, B. F. (1976) *About behaviorism.* New York: Vintage Books.

Sunstein, C. R. (2019) *Conformity: the power of social influence.* New York University Press.

Tallis, R. (2011) *Aping mankind: neuromania, Darwinitis and the misrepresentation of humanity.* Acumen.

Taylor, C. (2010) *Divas and door slammers: the secrets to having a better behaved teenager.* Random House.

Thaler, R. H. (2015) *Misbehaving: the making of behavioral economics.* W. W. Norton & Company.

Thaler, R. H., Sunstein, C. R. (2008) *Nudge: improving decisions about health, wealth, and happiness.* New Haven: Yale University Press.

Simler, K. and Hanson, R. (2018) *The elephant in the brain: hidden motives in everyday life.* Oxford University Press.

Trivers, R. (2013) *Deceit and self-deception: fooling yourself the better to fool others.* Penguin Books.

Robinson, M. (2013) *Trivium 21c: preparing young people for the future with lessons from the past.* Crown House Publishing.

Watson, P. (1978) *War on the mind: the military uses and abuses of psychology.* Pelican Books.

Whiting, R. (1987) *Crime and punishment: a study across time.* Stanley Thornes.

Wiliam, D. (2016) *Leadership for teacher learning: creating a culture where all teachers improve so that all students succeed.* Learning Sciences International.

Wiliam, D. (2018) *Creating the schools our children need.* Learning Sciences International.

Willingham, D. T. (2010) *Why don't students like school? A cognitive scientist answers questions about how the mind works and what it means for your classroom.* San Francisco, CA: Jossey-Bass.

Willingham, D. T. (2012) *When can you trust the experts? How to tell good science from bad in education.* Jossey-Bass.

INDEX